Explorings

EXPLORINGS

A collection of poems for
the young people of southern Africa

Compiled by Robin Malan

DAVID PHILIP
Cape Town and Johannesburg

First published 1988 in southern Africa by David Philip, Publisher (Pty) Ltd, 217 Werdmuller Centre, Claremont, 7700, South Africa

ISBN 0 86486 079 X

Printed by Clyson Printers (Pty) Ltd, 11th Avenue, Maitland, Cape, South Africa

Contents

"There are some really good moments . . ."

"Who's my neighbour?"

"What else shares the earth?"

"Not everyone thinks – or is – the same"

"It's a good feeling to be in love"

"Sometimes the place you're in makes a difference"

"There're some interesting people around"

"You get one helluva fright"

"Being a kid was fun . . ."

" . . . Not for everyone, though"

"Some of the people you meet . . . "

"So who's free?"

"What kind of world is this, then?"

"Who lets this kind of thing happen?"

Some words by way of explanation

It seems to me that there is a very interesting – almost paradoxical – stage that young people go through. At one and the same time, you're really concerned about other young people, about other people in general, and about what's going on around you and in the world out there. Yet it's also a time of intense self-involvement, sometimes to the apparent exclusion of everyone and everything else. Perhaps nowhere is this sense of 'Who am I?' and 'Where do I fit in?' more urgent and complicated than in Southern Africa now.

None of that's a startlingly original idea – though perhaps its application to all the young people in Southern Africa is more pressing than for young people elsewhere. Nor is the general phenomenon really all that surprising. It's during this time of your life that you need to decide who and what you are, and that decision can really only be made against a background of others: your family, your friends, your neighbours, your people, other people, places, animals, the world, the things you think, the things you feel, the things you believe in, the causes you intend to commit yourself to.

Now, poetry is about all of those things. And so, put young people and the right mix of poems together, and something good is bound to come out of it. The field is very wide, of course, and so any compiler has to decide what limits to impose. I've decided to choose poems that seem to fit in terms of time and place. Most of the poems were written fairly recently. Many of the poems come out of a Southern African experience. It's my hope that all of them could be useful in introducing the young people of Southern Africa to one another, as well as to people from elsewhere.

The poems are very loosely grouped under fairly tentative headings, but that's not to straitjacket the way the book is used. It's to suggest that some quite interesting things emerge if you juxtapose, contrast, compare, weigh up, see from different angles . . .

It's been a good experience to put the collection together. I hope that young people in Southern Africa find that it matches their needs, interests and concerns.

–RM, Mbabane, Swaziland

"You have to decide for yourself"

Robert Frost *USA, 1875–1964*

THE ROAD NOT TAKEN

Two roads diverged in a yellow wood,
And sorry I could not travel both
And be one traveler, long I stood
And looked down one as far as I could
To where it bent in the undergrowth;

Then took the other, as just as fair,
And having perhaps the better claim,
Because it was grassy and wanted wear;
Though as for that, the passing there
Had worn them really about the same,

And both that morning equally lay
In leaves no step had trodden black.
Oh, I kept the first for another day!
Yet knowing how way leads on to way,
I doubted if I should ever come back.

I shall be telling this with a sigh
Somewhere ages and ages hence:
Two roads diverged in a wood, and I—
I took the one less traveled by,
And that has made all the difference.

Obviously, the next piece is written as prose and not as verse. But it does raise questions about what a poem is. What does the word 'poetic' mean? Does a poem have to be written in shortish lines and in stanzas to qualify as a poem? Is this piece what can be called a 'prose-poem'? In the end, is what *it's saying more important than* how *it's saying it?*

Charles Rom *South Africa, b. 1949*

HOW SHALL I TELL?

How shall I tell of a confounded youth who saw not youth but a thousand monsters of another time—the septic sores of a too-strange world—with eyes unwidened to his fellows' joy; who built towers to the sky, which crashed at the touch of a steel-cold thought; who saw not beauty where other men walked, but the dull blankness of their animal minds; who saw too much of that which was real, and could not live with what he saw?

How shall I tell of a fragrant youth who slept wrapt 'tween mountain and sea on a soft pillow of the sweetest grass, with the stars all above him and a girl by his side who smelled of the early morning and whose hair was as light as a silken cloud and whose breath was warm on his cheek? And of how, with time-greased hands, he reached out to hold the night forever—and found that it was gone?

How shall I tell of a thousand thoughts which bubbled and fumed in his pent mind with no outlet to anything other than a world of fantasy where none could go save he? And who shall know of loneliness as he who knew a thousand men?

How shall I tell of a child who wished never to be a man; who feared the passing of childhood as the murderer fears the rope; who would have no part of growing old with nothing to clutch—whether it be Christ or a teddy-bear; who was too clever to believe in God and too foolish to believe in himself?

How shall I tell of a choking joy which lifted him up to walk on the clouds; which ballooned his soul and possessed his mind; which had nor face nor reason; which soon grew thin and faded away, for there was none with whom it might be shared?

How shall I tell of all these things? How shall I capture thoughts which race and fly too fast for any pen to frame? And who shall know of foolishness and love and hate and tears?

How then shall I tell of me?

Disturbances and confrontations with police, that eventually left about 700 young people dead, broke out in Soweto on 16 June 1976.

Fhazel Johennesse *South Africa, b. 1956*

A YOUNG MAN'S THOUGHTS BEFORE JUNE THE 16TH

tomorrow i travel on a road
that winds to the top of the hill
i take with me only the sweet
memories of my youth
my heart aches for my mother
for friday nights with friends
around a table with the broad belch of beer
i ask only for a sad song
sung by a woman with downturned eyes
and strummed by an old man with
a broken brow
o sing my sad song sing for me
for my sunset is drenched with red

The word 'catharsis' in the title of the next poem means, basically, 'getting it out of your system' and feeling the better for it.

Chris van Wyk *South Africa, b. 1957*

CATHARSIS

Sometimes during long silences
after emotional conversation
about the tenses in our lives
you suddenly lift your head from lifelines
and say:

There were times, Chris
when I wished I was the only child
Then there would've been enough food
to go round.

God how my friend can say things
we all felt at times
but rather left unsaid.

Motshile Nthodi *South Africa, b. 1948*

STANDARD FIFTY-EIGHT

Born on Saturday,
nineteen forty-eight.
After eight years,
my mother bought me a
        cheap slate for eight pence
        and took me to school.

Monday to Friday
in black and white,
from eight to two o'clock,
we planted tomatoes
and played football.

At the age of eighteen,
I passed standard eight
and became Baas Groen's
        good garden boy.

Today I'm twenty-eight
        years old,
        reading form fourteen,
        working in a garage,
        easy job—
                petrol attendant
for eight rands per month,
        easy job.

I wish I could pass standard
        fifty-eight,
                in cooking
        and become Mrs Beach's
        careless kitchen boy,
for eight cents per week.

Oh!
What an easy job.

You really need to see the Marc Chagall painting referred to in the next poem to appreciate the poem completely. Perhaps you can find a reproduction of it in a library.

Lawrence Ferlinghetti *USA, b. 1919*

DON'T LET THAT HORSE

Don't let that horse
                        eat that violin

    cried Chagall's mother

                              But he
                kept right on
                              painting

And became famous

And kept on painting
                        The Horse With Violin In Mouth
And when he finally finished it
he jumped up upon the horse
                              and rode away
    waving the violin

And then with a low bow gave it
to the first naked nude he ran across

And there were no strings
                              attached

Seamus Heaney *UK, b. 1939*

DIGGING

Between my finger and my thumb
The squat pen rests; snug as a gun.

Under my window, a clean rasping sound
When the spade sinks into gravelly ground:
My father, digging. I look down

Till his straining rump among the flowerbeds
Bends low, comes up twenty years away
Stooping in rhythm through potato drills
Where he was digging.

The coarse boot nestled on the lug, the shaft
Against the inside knee was levered firmly.
He rooted out tall tops, buried the bright edge deep
To scatter new potatoes that we picked
Loving their cool hardness in our hands.

By God, the old man could handle a spade.
Just like his old man.

My grandfather cut more turf in a day
Than any other man on Toner's bog.
Once I carried him milk in a bottle
Corked sloppily with paper. He straightened up
To drink it, then fell to right away
Nicking and slicing neatly, heaving sods
Over his shoulder, going down and down
For the good turf. Digging.

The cold smell of potato mould, the squelch and slap
Of soggy peat, the curt cuts of an edge
Through living roots awaken in my head.
But I've no spade to follow men like them.

Between my finger and my thumb
The squat pen rests.
I'll dig with it.

Gary Snyder *USA, b. 1930*

HAY FOR THE HORSES

He had driven half the night
From far down San Joaquin
Through Mariposa, up the
Dangerous mountain roads,
And pulled in at eight a.m.
With his big truckload of hay behind the barn.
With winch and ropes and hooks
We stacked the bales up clean
To splintery redwood rafters
High in the dark, flecks of alfalfa
Whirling through shingle-cracks of light,
Itch of haydust in the sweaty shirt and shoes.
At lunchtime under Black oak
Out in the hot corral,
—The old mare nosing lunchpails,
Grasshoppers crackling in the weeds—
'I'm sixty-eight,' he said,
'I first bucked hay when I was seventeen.
I thought, that day I started,
I sure would hate to do this all my life.
And dammit, that's just what
I've gone and done.'

“You have to think of your family”

Mazisi Kunene *South Africa, b. 1930*

IN PRAISE OF THE ANCESTORS

Even now the Forefathers still live
They are not overcome by the power of the whirlwind.
The day that sealed their eyes did not conquer them.
Even the tall boulder that stands over them
Casts only a humble shadow over their resting place.
They are the great voice that carries the epics.
The Ancestors have come to listen to our songs,
Overjoyed they shake their heads in ecstasy.
With us they celebrate their eternal life.
They climb the mountain with their children
To put the symbol of the ancient stone on its forehead.
We honour those who gave birth to us,
With them we watch the spectacle of the moving mists.
They have opened their sacred book to sing with us.
They are the mystery that envelops our dream.
They are the power that shall unite us.
They are the strange truth of the earth.
They came from the womb of the universe.
Restless they arc, like a path of dreams,
Like a forest sheltering the neighbouring race of animals.
Yes, the deep eye of the universe is in our chest.
With it we stare at the centres of the sky.
We sing the anthems that celebrate their great eras,
For indeed life does not begin with us.

Modikwe Dikobe *South Africa, b. 1913*

KHOIKHOI-SON-OF-MAN

I thought I was soul and skin
Pedigree muntu
Until yesterday I heard the truth
Grandfather was a Khoisan.

A slave of a trekboer
Fleeing from the Cape laws
Freeing slaves.

At night
He was tied to an oxwagon wheel
Groaning
Day by day leading sixteen span
Fleeing from the Cape.

Night by night
Somewhere there was a cock-crow
A barking dog
A smell of damp fuel
Then he realized that beyond that ridge
Could be a village
Of people like him.

He unfastened himself,
Trotted out of the camp,
Vanished into the night.

At dawn he was at a village
Begging to be taken into the tribe
        'A tribesman, hunter, chief's servant and messenger.'

Swift as an antelope was he
Outstripping runners
Chased by dogs.
        'Ka modimo,' they swore.
        'He is a man of the cloud.
        Ompone ke tswa kae?'
A legendary tale: where have you seen me?
        'I have seen you from the cloud.'
Khoikhoi-Son-of-Man.

I knew since yesterday
that he was my grandfather
Khoikhoi-Son-of-Man.

Magoleng wa Selepe *South Africa*

MY NAME
Nomgqibelo Ncamisile Mnqhibisa

Look what they have done to my name . . .
the wonderful name of my great-great-grandmothers
Nomgqibelo Ncamisile Mnqhibisa

The burly bureaucrat was surprised.
What he heard was music to his ears
'Wat is daai, sê nou weer?'
'I am from Chief Daluxolo Velayigodle of emaMpodweni
And my name is *Nomgqibelo Ncamisile Mnqhibisa.'*

Messia, help me!
My name is so simple
and yet so meaningful,
but to this man it is trash . . .

He gives me a name
Convenient enough to answer his whim:
I end up being
Maria . . .
I . . .
Nomgqibelo Ncamisile Mnqhibisa.

Jon Stallworthy *UK, b. 1935*

THE ALMOND TREE

I

All the way to the hospital
the lights were green as peppermints.
Trees of black iron broke into leaf
ahead of me, as if
I were the lucky prince
in an enchanted wood
summoning summer with my whistle,
banishing winter with a nod.

Swung by the road from bend to bend,
I was aware that blood was running
down through the delta of my wrist
and under arches
of bright bone. Centuries,
continents it had crossed;
from an undisclosed beginning
spiralling to an unmapped end.

II

Crossing (at sixty) Magdalen Bridge
Let it be a son, a son, said
the man in the driving mirror,
Let it be a son. The tower
held up its hand: the college
bells shook their blessing on his head.

III

I parked in an almond's
shadow blossom, for the tree
was waving, waving me
upstairs with a child's hands.

IV

Up
the spinal stair

and at the top
along
a bone-white corridor
the blood tide swung
me swung me to a room
whose walls shuddered
with the shuddering womb.

Under the sheet
wave after wave, wave
after wave beat
on the bone coast, bringing
ashore—whom?
                    New-
minted, my bright farthing!
Coined by our love, stamped with
our images, how you
enrich us! Both
you make one. Welcome
to your white sheet,
my best poem!

V

At seven-thirty
the visitors' bell
scissored the calm
of the corridors.
The doctor walked with me
to the slicing doors.
His hand upon my arm,
his voice—*I have to tell*
you—set another bell
beating in my head:
your son is a mongol
the doctor said.

VI

How easily the word went in—
clean as a bullet
leaving no mark on the skin,
stopping the heart within it.

This was my first death.
The 'I' ascending on a slow
last thermal breath
studied the man below
as a pilot treading air might
the buckled shell of his plane—
boot, glove, and helmet
feeling no pain

from the snapped wires' radiant ends.
Looking down from a thousand feet
I held four walls in the lens
of an eye; wall, window, the street

a torrent of windscreens, my own
car under its almond tree,
and the almond waving me down.
I wrestled against gravity,
but light was melting and the gulf
cracked open. Unfamiliar
the body of my late self
I carried to the car.

VII

The hospital—its heavy freight
lashed down ship-shape ward over ward—
steamed into night with some on board
soon to be lost if the desperate

charts were known. Others would come
altered to land or find the land
altered. At their voyage's end
some would be added to, some

diminished. In a numbered cot
my son sailed from me; never to come
ashore into my kingdom
speaking my language. Better not

look that way. The almond tree
was beautiful in labour. Blood-
dark, quickening, bud after bud
split, flower after flower shook free.

On the darkening wind a pale
face floated. Out of reach. Only when
the buds, all the buds, were broken
would the tree be in full sail.

In labour the tree was becoming
itself. I, too, rooted in earth
and ringed by darkness, from the death
of myself saw myself blossoming,

wrenched from the caul of my thirty
years' growing, fathered by my son,
unkindly in a kind season
by love shattered and set free.

VIII

You turn to the window for the first time.
I am called to the cot
to see your focus shift,
take tendril-hold on a shaft
of sun, explore its dusty surface, climb
to an eye you cannot

meet. You have a sickness they cannot heal,
the doctors say: locked in
your body you will remain.
Well, I have been locked in mine.
We will tunnel each other out. You seal
the covenant with a grin.

In the days we have known one another,
my little mongol love,
I have learnt more from your lips
than you will from mine perhaps:
I have learnt that to live is to suffer,
to suffer is to live.

Sipho Sepamla *South Africa, b. 1932*

THE FIRST BIRTHDAY

We salute this day
Making it two salutes for you

We tried to fuss with cakes and drinks
Thinking it a princely moment for you

We were about to sing praises
Wishing you the very best of futures

Then we saw you were bored with us
As if you knew days are the same
We saw you shrug us off
As if you knew life is that way

We felt like strangers in your company
Worrying about you, you playing as always
As if you were aware of a truth
We were hesitant to look in the eye

Then we checked this mockery of the day
To wish for you in the silence of the house:
    a sun that casts no shadows
    a living without distances
    a life of evergreen trees
    a world without fears

May the gods bless you with more
These birthdays we can't always remember
Happy Birthday to you!

See the poem Frieda's mother, Sylvia Plath, wrote about her, p. 129

Ted Hughes *UK, b. 1930*

FULL MOON AND LITTLE FRIEDA

A cool small evening shrunk to a dog bark and the clank of a
bucket–

And you listening.
A spider's web, tense for the dew's touch.
A pail lifted, still and brimming–mirror
To tempt a first star to a tremor.

Cows are going home in the lane there, looping the hedges with
their warm wreaths of breath–
A dark river of blood, many boulders,
Balancing unspilled milk.

'Moon!' you cry suddenly, 'Moon! Moon!'

The moon has stepped back like an artist gazing amazed at a work

That points at him amazed.

Adam Small *South Africa, b. 1936*

BROWN LULLABY

They call your mama girl
love
they call your mama girl
all places that she go
they call your mama girl
they see to all the white man first
your mama she must wait
your mama she must wait very long
afore they call her girl
but your mama she come home
love

your mama she come home
for nothin' but to love you
your mama she come home
an' she love you more than she got to wait
aye even more
an' more to-day than yesterday
more everyday

Dannie Abse *UK, b. 1923*

DRIVING HOME

Opposing carbeams wash my face.
Such flickerings hypnotise. To keep awake
I listen to the BBC through cracklings
of static, fade-outs under bridges,
to a cool expert who, in lower case,
computes and graphs 'the ecological
disasters that confront the human race.'

Almost immediately (ironically?),
I see blue flashing lights ahead and brake
before a car accordioned, floodlit, men heaving
at a stretcher, an ambulance oddly angled, tame, in wait.
Afterwards, silent, I drive home cautiously
where, late, the eyes of my youngest child
flicker dreamily, and are full of television.

'He's waited up,' his mother says, 'to say goodnight.'
My son smiles briefly. Such emotion! I surprise
myself and him when I hug him tight.

C Day Lewis *UK, 1904–1974*

WALKING AWAY

For Sean

It is eighteen years ago, almost to the day—
A sunny day with the leaves just turning,
The touch-lines new-ruled—since I watched you play
Your first game of football, then, like a satellite
Wrenched from its orbit, go drifting away

Behind a scatter of boys. I can see
You walking away from me towards the school
With the pathos of a half-fledged thing set free
Into a wilderness, the gait of one
Who finds no path where the path should be.

That hesitant figure, eddying away
Like a winged seed loosened from its parent stem,
Has something I never quite grasp to convey
About nature's give-and-take—the small, the scorching
Ordeals which fire one's irresolute clay.

I have had worse partings, but none that so
Gnaws at my mind still. Perhaps it is roughly
Saying what God alone could perfectly show—
How selfhood begins with a walking away,
And love is proved in the letting go.

Charles Mungoshi *Zimbabwe, b. 1947*

A LETTER TO A SON

Now the pumpkin is ripe.
We are only a few days from
the year's first mealie cob.
The cows are giving us lots of milk.
Taken in the round it isn't a bad year at all—

if it weren't for your father.
Your father's back is back again
and all the work has fallen on my shoulders.
Your little brothers and sisters are doing
fine at the day-school. Only Rindai
is becoming a problem. You will remember
we wrote you—did you get our letter?—
you didn't answer—you see, since your
father's back started we haven't been able
to raise enough to send your sister Rindai
to secondary school. She spends most of the time
crying by the well. It's mainly because of her
that I am writing this letter.
I had thought you would be with us last Christmas
then I thought maybe you were too busy
and you would make it at Easter—
it was then your father nearly left us, son.
Then I thought I would come to you some time
before the cold season settled in—you know how
I simply hate that time of year—
but then your father went down again
and this time worse than any other time before.
We were beginning to think he would never see
another sowing season. I asked your sister Rindai
to write you but your father would have none of it
—you know how stubborn he can get when
he has to lie in bed all day or gets
one of those queer notions of his that
everybody is deserting him!
Now, Tambu, don't think I am asking for money—
although we had to borrow a little from
those who have it to get your father to hospital
and you know how he hates having to borrow!
That is all I wanted to tell you.
I do hope that you will be with us this July.
It's so long ago since we last heard from you—
I hope this letter finds you still at the old address.
It is the only address we know.

YOUR MOTHER

Langston Hughes *USA, 1902–1967*

MOTHER TO SON

Well, son, I'll tell you.
Life for me ain't been no crystal stair.
It's had tacks in it,
And splinters,
And boards torn up,
And bare places with no carpet on the floor . . .
Bare.
But all the time
I'se been a-climbin' on,
And reachin' landin's
And turnin' corners,
And sometimes goin' in the dark
Where there ain't been no light.
So, boy, don't you turn back.
Don't you set down on the steps
'Cause you'll find it kinder hard.
Don't you fall now . . .
For I'se still goin', honey,
I'se still climbin',
And life for me ain't been no crystal stair.

Jennifer Davids *South Africa, b. 1945*

POEM FOR MY MOTHER

That isn't everything, you said
on the afternoon I brought a poem
to you hunched over the washtub
with your hands
the shrivelled
burnt granadilla
skin of your hands
covered by foam.

And my words
slid like a ball
of hard blue soap
into the tub
to be grabbed and used by you
to rub the clothes.

A poem isn't all
there is to life, you said
with your blue-ringed gaze
scanning the page
once looking over my shoulder
and back at the immediate
dirty water

and my words
being clenched
smaller and
smaller.

Andrew Waterman *UK, b. 1940*

MOTHER

I should be grateful. You
adopted me in a hard time,
the sound of guns from Dunkirk shaking
London, the bombs. You have told
how once you lay over my pram as a German
aeroplane swooped to machine-gun the street.
What made you, you never did say.

It was only 'You should be grateful' became
the theme you played on a subtle keyboard
(you'd not been an actress in vain):
grateful for supper, for half-days in Brighton,
for wellington boots in rainy weather,
'For all I have done for you.'
There was also your tone saying 'Don't.'

And when father left you said nothing,
except—remember?—when
I finally asked, that day in the park
at the rusted green cafeteria seats,
to distract me, 'Look at those sparrows,'
and did not notice rage boiling the dregs
of a nine-year-old's childhood away.

So I locked you from me in turn, as I locked
my schoolwork away in a case.
Where was I going? 'Out.'
And when leaving for good I came
to tell you, you carried on hanging up washing,
not taking the peg from your mouth, just said
'Remember to leave your doorkey.'

At seventy now, arthritis
has withered the touch and range
from your piano-player's hands,
your first teeth are gone (years after mine).
Hoarding a fossil faith
in Stalin, the god that failed,
you keep up the garden, read Dickens, see plays,

and we can be easier together,
and I am truly grateful.
If what you pinched and scraped once seemed
me, I know now it was for me,
understand things you still cannot say
as your talkative letters come, each signed
not 'with love,' just 'as ever'.

Robert Greig *South Africa, b. 1948*

THE RACE

I still remember that hot Sunday–
Squinting at my father in the sun
While he captured winds in a curve of sail,
And the yacht–squat, old, capricious–
Creaking as she butted towards
The rock-face. I waited for the crack
And rattle of canvas as we went about.

The rock-face loomed, and water leapt
To my toes. Shouldn't we go about, Dad?'
I was too timid at 12 to call.
I clung to rope and watched him:
Lips drawn back, knuckles whitening,
Eyeless behind his sunlensed spectacles.
Still the sheet-rock grew and still
He smiled. As I yelled 'Dad',
Wind and rope snatched the glasses.

One hand groped for glasses
Drifting down to the mud.
I saw he could not see
The brown, leering rocks or
My terrified face as he blinked.

I forget what happened next.
I know we went about in time,
But did not win the race.
We returned to the club-house, Dad
Cursing his luck, and I shocked
By the facts of scrabbling fingers,
His unguarded sockets.

Under South African legislation, when a person is declared a 'banned person', he may not attend a social gathering; and a gathering is defined as 'more than one other person'.

Hugh Lewin *South Africa, b. 1939*

THE WEDDING

Solly Nathee
stood alone
on the koppie overlooking his home.

Solly Nathee
alone on the koppie
stood watching his home
where his daughter was getting married.

The guests
at the home below
were feasting the bride and the groom.

Near Solly Nathee
on the koppie
sat the Special Branch
watching
to see that Solly Nathee
banned from social gatherings
behaved himself
at his daughter's wedding.

The guests
at the home below
feasted the bride and the groom
then walked
one by one
up the koppie
to shake the hand of Solly Nathee.

Solly Nathee
at his daughter's wedding
stood on the koppie overlooking his home
alone.

Seamus Heaney *UK, b. 1939*

FOLLOWER

My father worked with a horse-plough,
His shoulders globed like a full sail strung
Between the shafts and the furrow.
The horses strained at his clicking tongue.

An expert. He would set the wing
And fit the bright steel-pointed sock.
The sod rolled over without breaking.
At the headrig, with a single pluck

Of reins, the sweating team turned round
And back into the land. His eye
Narrowed and angled at the ground,
Mapping the furrow exactly.

I stumbled in his hob-nailed wake,
Fell sometimes on the polished sod;
Sometimes he rode me on his back
Dipping and rising to his plod.

I wanted to grow up and plough,
To close one eye, stiffen my arm.
All I ever did was follow
In his broad shadow round the farm.

I was a nuisance, tripping, falling,
Yapping always. But today
It is my father who keeps stumbling
Behind me, and will not go away.

Ridley Beeton *South Africa, b. 1929*

AUTUMN

Patterns of old green-gold trees,
Patterns of aloes dipped in blood;

The khaki veld hums, a long singing
Late-noon dream. And I shall come

Up to the house and its purple shades,
And talk to my father, and he will
Tell me of the world that has been,
And I shall tell him of the world

That will come, and he will tell me
That it is wrong, wrong, and I
Shall think that he is wrong, old and wrong.
But when I emerge into the khaki veld

And feel the fine air stabbing out at me,
And the night that is sweeping up
Across the world, I shall sometimes
Think that he is right, young and right.

ON THE BEACH
(for my father)

He lay quietly on the bed,
His hands huge, vegetably still.
Only his eyes turned as I came in
And came to his side, to say 'hullo'.

Ridiculously, that was all I could say
To a man who had loomed, like God, in my life.
It was such an important time, and all I could say,
With a nurse-like informality, was 'Hullo', and then
'How are you?'

My heart should have melted, I should have enclosed
him in my love;
But I sat, stilted and stiff, watching the timeless clock.
It was not that at the last he meant little. He meant
much:
How does one give life to a hugeness which makes one
so small?

I wanted to do for him everything that I could,
Because life (his life) was a big thing.
I did not want the leaving of it to be mean.
I wanted to bring him so many things:
I wanted to bring religion, comfort, the cool of ice (in
my warmth).

I sat helplessly, hard and withdrawn, as he suffered
away into the sea of death,
Which I could see splashing its waves over his face.

Dylan Thomas *UK, 1914–1953*

DO NOT GO GENTLE INTO THAT GOOD NIGHT

Do not go gentle into that good night,
Old age should burn and rave at close of day;
Rage, rage against the dying of the light.

Though wise men at their end know dark is right,
Because their words had forked no lightning they
Do not go gentle into that good night.

Good men, the last wave by, crying how bright
Their frail deeds might have danced in a green bay,
Rage, rage against the dying of the light.

Wild men who caught and sang the sun in flight,
And learn, too late, they grieved it on its way,
Do not go gentle into that good night.

Grave men, near death, who see with blinding sight
Blind eyes could blaze like meteors and be gay,
Rage, rage against the dying of the light.

And you, my father, there on the sad height,
Curse, bless, me now with your fierce tears, I pray.
Do not go gentle into that good night.
Rage, rage against the dying of the light.

e e cummings *USA, 1894–1962*

NOBODY LOSES ALL THE TIME

nobody loses all the time

i had an uncle named
Sol who was a born failure and
nearly everybody said he should have gone
into vaudeville perhaps because my Uncle Sol could
sing McCann He Was A Diver on Xmas Eve like Hell Itself which
may or may not account for the fact that my Uncle

Sol indulged in that possibly most inexcusable
of all to use a highfalootin phrase
luxuries that is or to
wit farming and be
it needlessly
added

my Uncle Sol's farm
failed because the chickens
ate the vegetables so
my Uncle Sol had a
chicken farm till the
skunks ate the chickens when

my Uncle Sol
had a skunk farm but
the skunks caught cold and
died and so
my Uncle Sol imitated the
skunks in a subtle manner

or by drowning himself in the watertank
but somebody who'd given my Uncle Sol a Victor
Victrola and records while he lived presented to
him upon the auspicious occasion of his decease a
scrumptious not to mention splendiferous funeral with
tall boys in black gloves and flowers and everything and

i remember we all cried like the Missouri
when my Uncle Sol's coffin lurched because
somebody pressed a button
(and down went
my Uncle
Sol

and started a worm farm)

William Carlos Williams *USA, 1883–1963*

THE LAST WORDS OF MY ENGLISH GRANDMOTHER

There were some dirty plates
and a glass of milk
beside her on a small table
near the rank, disheveled bed—

Wrinkled and nearly blind
she lay and snored
rousing with anger in her tones
to cry for food,

Gimme something to eat—
They're starving me—
I'm all right I won't go
to the hospital. No, no, no

Give me something to eat.
Let me take you
to the hospital, I said
and after you are well

you can do as you please.
She smiled, Yes
you do what you please first
then I can do what I please—

Oh,oh, oh! she cried
as the ambulance men lifted
her to the stretcher–
Is this what you call

making me comfortable?
By now her mind was clear–
Oh you think you're smart
you young people,

she said, but I'll tell you
you don't know anything.
Then we started.
On the way

we passed a long row
of elms. She looked at them
awhile out of
the ambulance window and said,

What are all those
fuzzy-looking things out there?
Trees? Well, I'm tired
of them and rolled her head away.

Keorapetse Kgositsile *South Africa, b. 1938*

THE ELEGANCE OF MEMORY

Distances separate bodies not people. Ask
Those who have known sadness or joy
The bone of feeling is pried open
By a song, the elegance
Of color, a familiar smell, this
Flower or the approach of an evening . . .

All this is NOW

I used to wonder
Was her grave warm enough,
'Madikeledi, my grandmother,

As big-spirited as she was big-legged,
She would talk to me. She would . . .
How could I know her sadness then
Or who broke my father's back?
But now . . .

The elegance of memory,
Deeper than the grave
Where she went before I could
Know her sadness, is larger
Than the distance between
My country and I. Things more solid
Than the rocks with which those sinister
Thieves tried to break our back

I hear her now. And I wonder
Now does she know the strength
of the fabric
She wove in my heart for us? . . . Her
Voice clearer now than then: Boykie,
Dont ever take any nonsense from them,
You hear!

Edwin Brock *UK, b. 1927*

A MOMENT OF RESPECT

Two things I remember about my grandfather:
his threadbare trousers, and the way he adjusted
his half-hunter watch two minutes every day.

When I asked him why he needed to know the time
so
exactly, he said a business man could lose a fortune
by being two minutes late for an appointment.

When he died he left two meerschaum pipes
and a golden sovereign on a chain. Somebody

threw the meerschaum pipes away, and
there was an argument about the sovereign.

On the day of his burial the church clock chimed
as he was lowered down into the clay, and all
the family advanced their watches by two minutes.

Musaemura Zimunya *Zimbabwe, b. 1949*

ASK GRANDPA

Ask Grandpa
he will tell you
he will educate you
ask him
ask him

who knows
why buses are
moving coffins
he knows
ask him
ask him

who knows
how the last lion
hid in a woman's womb
and came out
in the form of a man
he knows
ask him
ask him

who knows
why cities are jungles
too tough for you
he knows
ask him
listen and ponder

"There are some really good moments . . ."

William Carlos Williams was a country doctor. Having come back home late after a night call, he left this note for his wife.

William Carlos Williams *USA, 1883–1963*

THIS IS JUST TO SAY

I have eaten
the plums
that were in
the icebox

and which
you were probably
saving
for breakfast

Forgive me
they were delicious
so sweet
and so cold

Gregory Corso *USA, b. 1930*

SECOND NIGHT IN NYC AFTER 3 YEARS

I was happy I was bubbly drunk
The street was dark
I waved to a young policeman
He smiled
I went up to him and like a flood of gold
Told him all about my prison youth
About how noble and great some convicts were
And about how I just returned from Europe
Which wasn't half as enlightening as prison
And he listened attentively I told no lie
Everything was truth and humor
He laughed

He laughed
And it made me so happy I said:
'Absolve it all, kiss me!'
'No no no no!' he said
and hurried away.

William Carlos Williams *USA, 1883–1963*

THE ARTIST

Mr. T.
bareheaded
in a soiled undershirt
his hair standing out
on all sides
stood on his toes
heels together
arms gracefully
for the moment
curled above his head.
Then he whirled about
bounded
into the air
and with an *entrechat*
perfectly achieved
completed the figure.
My mother
taken by surprise
where she sat
in her invalid's chair
was left speechless.
Bravo! she cried at last
and clapped her hands.
The man's wife
came from the kitchen:
What goes on here? she said.
But the show was over.

Wopko Jensma *South Africa, b. 1939*

from

NOT HIM

3

he forbids us to dance
he always leads the church service
he has a stable job
he is always on time for work
he never gets drunk
he has respect for most people
everybody respects him
we love our daddy
but sometimes i notice
when a kwela blasts from the radio
he wiggles his toes

Michele Freind *South Africa*

DAYS

wednesday is dreamday
dullday tiredday
need a holiday
thinking of saturday

saturday is stanleyday
townday dateday
needed a funday
thinking of sunday

sunday is sleepday
beachday eatday
needed a coolday
thinking of schoolday

e e cummings *USA, 1894–1962*

I THANK YOU GOD FOR MOST THIS AMAZING

i thank You God for most this amazing
day:for the leaping greenly spirits of trees
and a blue true dream of sky;and for everything
which is natural which is infinite which is yes

(i who have died am alive again today,
and this is the sun's birthday;this is the birth
day of life and of love and wings:and of the gay
great happening illimitably earth)

how should tasting touching hearing seeing
breathing any–lifted from the no
of all nothing–human merely being
doubt unimaginable You?

(now the ears of my ears awake and
now the eyes of my eyes are opened)

Robert Frost *USA, 1875–1964*

A TIME TO TALK

When a friend calls to me from the road
And slows his horse to a meaning walk,
I don't stand still and look around
On all the hills I haven't hoed,
And shout from where I am, 'What is it?'
No, not as there is a time to talk.
I thrust my hoe in the mellow ground,
Blade-end up and five feet tall,
And plod: I go up to the stone wall
For a friendly visit.

Douglas Dunn *UK, b. 1942*

LATE NIGHT WALK DOWN TERRY STREET

A policeman on a low-powered motorcycle stops.
His radio crackles, his helmet yellows.

Empty buses heading for the depot
Rush past the open end of Terry Street.

In their light, a man with a bike walking home,
Too drunk to ride it, turns into Terry Street.

Taxis swerve down Terry Street's shortcut,
Down uneven halls of Street Lighting Department yellow.

Into which now comes the man with the bike,
Struggling to keep on his legs.

The policeman waits under a gone-out streetlamp.
He stops the drunk, they talk, they laugh together.

I pass them then, beside dark, quiet houses,
In others mumbling sounds of entertainment;

Cathode-glows through curtains, faint latest tunes;
Creaking of bedsprings, lights going out.

Damian Ruth *South Africa, b. 1954*

WHEN I GO HOME

When I go home
I'm going to find
a stretch of road
in the Karroo
that lies flat and straight for miles.
I will come
over the crest of a koppie
and in the distance see
the windmill and its reservoir
next to the road.

I'll sit on the koppie
and look at it.
On the other side of the earth
under the huge pale blue sky
will be a thin line of purple koppies.
Eventually
I'll hear the insects scratching
and maybe a hot exhausted stone
finally splitting.

I'll walk slowly
towards the windmill,
sometimes on the sticky black asphalt
sometimes next to it,
kicking stones
and lifting puffs of dust.
I'll climb through
the barbwire fence,
strip naked
and swim in the reservoir.
I'll sit in the sun to dry.
After a while
I'll climb back
through the barbwire fence
onto the road again.

I lived in South Africa
for 25 years
and never did that once.

Chris van Wyk *South Africa, b. 1957*

ON LEARNING SOTHO
(for Isaac Sephoka)

I was a young Sotho boy then
a baby wetting a layette of words
and all of you laughed boisterously
when I swore at myself
not knowing the difference then
between 'nna' and 'wena'.
And I'd impress all the ladies
with 'dumela ausi!'
or 'moratiwa!' when I was randy.

The words crawled at first
no matter how they tried to walk
among the grown, bombastic men.
Oh I was a child again
joyfully sucking on the tits
of a language new to me
though it had always been
dangling invitingly from Agnes who makes the tea
or Mrs Mabuja who sweeps the office.

Thank you for your patience brother
and your English to guide my Sotho.
I'm growing now
and one day I will be as big as you
and Joseph and Walter and Lucky.
Then I will also laugh when you do
or cry
and understand why.

Peter Strauss *South Africa, b. 1941*

from
BUSHMAN WOMAN EATS A TSAMA MELON

1

The fingers find a journey
From the melon to the mouth–

A straightest path
Among many invariables:

> Eye canting on the head's lunge
> Structure of the hand and arm
> Arc and pivot of the elbow
> Adaptabilities of the wrist–

In fact, the rhythms of eating.

Between her and the melon
It is a question of give and take.
And when she takes it in,
She gives herself up to the taking.

2

She gives herself up to the tasting
With an energy that drags on her own skin

Collapses the back of her hand in drawn sinews
So she can get it all in, all of it,
In her round mouth curved for pleasure

She sucks till the blood moves in her fingers
To join the juice of the melon

She tastes herself in tasting

"Who's my neighbour?"

Stephen Spender *UK, b. 1909*

MY PARENTS KEPT ME FROM CHILDREN WHO WERE ROUGH

My parents kept me from children who were rough
And who threw words like stones and who wore torn
clothes.
Their thighs showed through rags. They ran in the street
And climbed cliffs and stripped by the country streams.

I feared more than tigers their muscles like iron
And their jerking hands and their knees tight on my arms.
I feared the salt coarse pointing of those boys
Who copied my lisp behind me on the road.

They were lithe, they sprang out behind hedges
Like dogs to bark at our world. They threw mud
And I looked another way, pretending to smile.
I longed to forgive them, yet they never smiled.

Henry Pote *Zimbabwe, b. 1939*

TO A WHITE CHILD

Your mother and father, eccentrics
And venturesome, made us friends.
You, innocent, guileless, saw no tricks
And always accepted my presence
With nonchalance and little wonder.
Something about my grins won you over,
You would constantly wait and hover
Till opportunity turned to tell your secret naive
About your doll, your prowess, and how you strive
And need my aid to reconstruct a broken toy.
Will your trust vanish when you grow older?
Will you think you alone can order?
It cannot be: you're already too wise
To somersault and move anti-clockwise.

Sol Rachilo *South Africa*

THE ANONYMOUS HOUSEBOY

The madam won't worry about shoes for me
no genuine cowhide needed
the soles of my feet are hard and sturdy
so why bother
but for a vintage collection
let me write home for Izimbadada.
The white tennis shoes
neat and slightly oversized
are my everyday footwear.
In them,
and inside my incredible
kitchen boy suit
that never fits too well,
(I prefer mine white
it makes me
look like a circus clown.)
But all the same I'm happy,
a free suit from the missus
it's as good as
a well earned bonsella.
I bathe poodles
and take fox terriers
for a walk in white suburbia.
Nobody knows me.
I occasionally meet
homeboys emptying the ashes
into dustbins.
It's a usual salutation:
'How's home?
Has your heifer yielded
anything this year?'
I stick to my strict duties.
Then there's a big fight at the flat
and the white Baas fires me.
I'll do the mine or

become a night watchman.
I'm satisfied
my children will not starve.

William Hussey *Zimbabwe, 1953–1977*

MAN SERVANT

He hits out–I dodge–laugh,
Rush to the kitchen.
He curses–I smile–run,
Scramble to the table.
I wash the plates–eat
The tasty scraps–and
He hates me–I the
Darker brother,

He knows he will soon
be gone.

I sit–eat his food
Grow strong on his milk
The fat of his household.
I read his books, smoke his cigars
Even sleep in his bed–Oh, and guess!
But really I do not care.

He knows he will soon
be gone.

So in the meantime
I laugh–idle about,
Sip fine brandy and
Dream of the sun
Tomorrow–
  When he will go.

Motshile Nthodi *South Africa, b. 1948*

SOUTH AFRICAN DIALOGUE

Morning Baas,
Baas,
Baas Kleinbaas says,
I must come and tell
Baas that,
Baas Ben's Baasboy says,
Baas Ben want to see
Baas Kleinbaas if
Baas don't use
Baas Kleinbaas,
Baas.

Tell
Baas Kleinbaas that,
Baas says,
Baas Kleinbaas must tell
Baas Ben's Baasboy that,
Baas Ben's Baasboy must tell
Baas Ben that,
Baas says,
If Baas Ben want to see
Baas Kleinbaas,
Baas Ben must come and see
Baas Kleinbaas here.

Thank you
Baas.
I'll tell
Baas Kleinbaas that,
Baas says,
Baas Kleinbaas must tell
Baas Ben's Baasboy that,
Baas Ben's Baasboy must tell
Baas Ben that,
Baas says,

If Baas Ben want to see
Baas Kleinbaas,
Baas Ben must come and see
Baas Kleinbaas here,
Baas
Goodbye Baas.

Baas Kleinbaas,
Baas says,
I must come and tell
Baas Kleinbaas that,
Baas Kleinbaas must tell
Baas Ben's Baasboy that,
Baas Ben's Baasboy must tell
Baas Ben that,
Baas says,
If Baas Ben want to see
Baas Kleinbaas,
Baas Ben must come and see
Baas Kleinbaas here,
Baas Kleinbaas.

Baasboy,
Tell Baas Ben that,
Baas Kleinbaas says,
Baas says,
If Baas Ben want to see me
(Kleinbaas),
Baas Ben must come and
See me (Kleinbaas) here.

Thank you
Baas Kleinbaas,
I'll tell
Baas Ben that,
Baas Kleinbaas says,
Baas says,
If Baas Ben want to see
Baas Kleinbaas,
Baas Ben must come and see

Baas Kleinbaas here,
Baas Kleinbaas.
Goodbye
Baas Kleinbaas.

Baas Ben,
Baas Kleinbaas says,
I must come and tell
Baas Ben that,
Baas says,
If Baas Ben want to see
Baas Kleinbaas,
Baas Ben must come and see
Baas Kleinbaas there,
Baas Ben.
Baas Ben,
Baas Be-ne . . . .
Baas Ben.
Goodbye
Baas Ben.

Mongane Serote *South Africa, b. 1944*

THE ACTUAL DIALOGUE

Do not fear Baas.
It's just that I appeared
And our faces met
In this black night that's like me.
Do not fear –
We will always meet
When you do not expect me.
I will appear
In the night that's black like me.
Do not fear–
Blame your heart
When you fear me–
I will blame my mind

When I fear you
In the night that's black like me.
Do not fear Baas,
My heart is vast as the sea
And your mind as the earth.
It's awright Baas,
Do not fear.

Mike Kirkwood *South Africa, b. 1943*

NEIGHBOURS

Over your shoulder you throw ropes
of raw earth down the scrub, snaring
the thickets in loops, letting down
tenuous travellers, herdboys, cows.

The vlei between us is no man's.

Vigilant, I pump in ten rounds
of golf ball a day, and patrol
my hillside for the spent casings.

The herdboys also play, with clubs
sawn-off and hickory-shafted,
teeing on tufts the balls I lose.

Back at home, I'm learning Zulu.
Radio Bantu at peak volume,
ready to receive your envoy.

You send down a *tsotsi* with a knife,
and call me at dusk to the vlei,

send down his interpreter, who squats
in a bloodied shirt explaining
a ten-cent slot under the heart,

the ambulance a long time coming.

A L Hendriks *West Indies*

NEIGHBOUR, TENTH FLOOR

Beyond a span of wall
        I can imagine you:

gaping
        your sleep-soured dawnbreaths,
waking
        your habitual body,
and in a web of bedclothes
sitting up
        dishevelled
to grope for clock and eyeglasses
as I reach out for mine.

I know you pace your cage,
halfway up to the sky
in this communal ivory tower,
for I hear your footsteps
echoing mine
        in the adjacent cell.

When you flush your waste
my cistern gurgles too,
and the mutter of my saucepans
answers the descant of yours.

Boxed in our hired cubicles
we act the self-same ings
feeding cursing waiting
and watching television
(that disingenuous window).

We nod civilly on thresholds,
grin cosily in liftcars,
and disappear
scuttling like land-crabs
into separate occasions.

Daily I want to rush to you
weeping with recognition
and embrace you calling,
calling,
            I am your neighbour
               Love me,

then live with you,
together away
            from these lonely dens;

but what would be the use?

It is better to tap out an endless message
against that imperceptible wall
that must always divide us.

It's fairly obvious from the next two poems that the writer, Bernard Levinson, is a psychiatrist. Perhaps not so obvious, the poet who follows after these two poems, Douglas Livingstone, is a marine bacteriologist. So, another prejudice is knocked on the head: that you need to be a particular 'type' to be a poet.

Bernard Levinson *South Africa, b. 1926*

GROUP THERAPY

We were talking about love
(not daring to use that word)
as they sat about me
in a circle.
The boys and the girls
each with a puppet on one hand.

He said–
'Mine's an old man.
He's so very hungry
and so very much alone.'
And she in the softest voice–
'My puppet's ugly
everyone hates her.'

I searched for words
to form a bridge
between them.

The old man looked at the ugly puppet.
The paper heads nodded gravely
while the group waited.

And I, groping in my word-world
waited for the right words
to set them free.

On an impulse,
he stretched forward
and gently swept her hair
out of her face.

YOUR SMALL FIST

There's no need for words.
Your small fist
cupped in the palm of my hand–
I insinuate a finger
inside the curled barricade–
and read the temperature,
the amount of hurt–
the hold-tight pain of your young life.

I remember once before–
my first call to the township
between the steaming huts
on the lip of a makeshift road

where I swung my black bag
brash as a boy
safe in his Medical School.

The dark girl in labour
was younger than I.
A child bearing a child.
I fumbled in my bag
looking for words
among the shoe-horn shapes,
the trumpets and the string.
In the end she cried
and I held her hand . . .

Douglas Livingstone *South Africa, b. 1932*

DUST

The bundle in the gutter had its skull
cracked open by a kierie.
The blunt end of a sharpened bicycle
spoke grew a solitary
silver war-plume from the nape of his neck.
I turned him gently. He'd thinned to a wreck.

It was my friend Mketwa. He was dead.
Young Mac the Knife, I'd called him,
without much originality. Red
oozed where they'd overhauled him.
An illegal five-inch switchblade, his 'best'
possession, was stuck sideways in his chest.

He had been tough; moved gracefully, with ease.
We'd bricked, built walls, carted sand;
pitting strength against cement-bags, we'd seize
and humpf, steadied by a hand.
I paid the regulation wage plus fifty
per cent, his room, his board. He wasn't thrifty.

We were extending the old house I'd bought.
Those baked-lung middays we'd swill
the dust with cans of ice-cold beer. I thought
he must be unkillable,
except by white men. Each night the beerhall
took him: stoned wide, he would not stall or fall.

I don't think he learnt anything tangible
from me. From him, I learnt much:
his mother, cattle, kraal; the terrible
cheat that repaired his watch; such
and such pleased a woman; passes; bus queues;
whereabouts to buy stolen nails and screws.

His wife in Kwa Mashu, a concubine
in Chesterville, a mistress
in town: all pregnant. He'd bought turpentine
but they wouldn't drink it. This
was the trouble with women. Letters came
we couldn't read. He found another dame.

He left—more money, walls half-done, him tight—
to join Ital-Constructions.
Perhaps it had been white men: I am white.
Now, I phoned the ambulance
and sat with him. It came for Mac the Knife;
bore his corpse away; not out of my life.

Modikwe Dikobe *South Africa, b. 1913*

GRAVE OF UNKNOWN WHITEMAN

Rest in peace, old man
A heap of rocks on your grave
Is a token of respect
Bestowed on you.

You chose this part of the country
For a home
On a slope of those rocks
Was your community
And across that road
You sowed corn
And watered your cattle in that pan.

In years of dearth
We shared together
Helped each other in time of need.

Rest in peace, old man
Your kindred are here
Paying due respect
Rest in peace!

"What else shares the earth?"

Michael Baldwin *UK, b. 1930*

HUNTING WITH A STICK

Once, ten years old, in the cobweb sun
I chased a rabbit on stiffening grass
Till it twinkled into its hole of sand.
Although I knew that the hunt was done
(For rabbits burrow deeper than fire)
I crouched and crept there, stretching my hand,
And kneeling my shadow on frost I saw
In a turn of the hole too tight to pass
Its fluffed fat haunches were firmly jammed,
Its white tail sat as still as a star.

The moment froze in a single breath:
Give me a second and I could be quick,
Having spent ten years in the ways of death,
And I wanted this death, not one planned.
I thrust at its buttocks with my stick
And felt the soft bone go under the fur,
The silence I knelt on echo and stir,
The green meat of mornings that made me sick . . .

I dragged it back by a fistful of hair,
Then flourished my prize with a dripping claw;
But dangling it upwards again I saw
Its face was bitten and muffled in blood,
One eye was empty and showed the skull,
The soft jaw was eaten into a snarl,
Death hung from its ears in a glistening hood.

And at ten years old I first understood
There were other deaths in the world than me,
More ways to kill than with stone and stick:
While my shadow falconed it from the air
A stoat had sat in its horror there
And bitten its burrowing bone to the quick.

Douglas Livingstone *South Africa, b. 1932*

A PIECE OF EARTH

The blue duiker, left hindleg
in a poacher's noose held
to a piece of earth by an iron peg,
stands, heart jumping, puzzled;
his scared velvet ears spread
to the sly rustle of leaves and stems;
huge tired eyes probing
the recesses of his epoch's dusk.

He has been snared three days
of sleepless terror; throat scorched with thirst,
tongue thick from rust, dust and blood,
one tiny horn broken from his first
fight with the iron in the earth's skin.
The footloose poacher, long gone
for weeks, has moved on,
will not be returning.

At lengthening intervals
the hare-sized buck gathers himself
for bounding, mouth wide and whistling,
to tow the piece of earth with him.
The wire bites tighter.
Blood flows, clots, runs, congeals
until metal wholly rings on bone.
The earth remains unmoving.

He stops aghast at his noise;
quivering, pants quietly;
resumes his frenzied leaping.
Soon, small herbivorous teeth
will have to grit to gnaw through pain.
Water lies a doubtful day
away: a three-legged stumble through
hyena-patrolled terrain.

D H Lawrence *UK, 1885–1930*

SELF-PITY

I never saw a wild thing
sorry for itself.
A small bird will drop frozen dead from a bough
without ever having felt sorry for itself.

Anthony Delius *South Africa, b. 1916*

THE THINKER

Round and round our lavatory
walks a depressed cricket
like a lonely manager
of a cement factory,

the huge cistern and bowl
and mysterious pipes above him,
and he worries, ticking with calculation,
troubled about production
and reproduction.

Every now and then, at unpredictable intervals,
comes darkness,
and seven-league boots, and enormous draperies
drop down from heaven,
and afterwards
a great roaring, an apocalypse of waters.

And the serpent holding the world
together unclenches its tail
and hisses—and boots and draperies
retreat reluctantly, thundering.

And the cricket thinks:
Well, there must be a rational explanation,
I suppose—but, all the same,
it seems bloody queer.

Jeremy Cronin *South Africa, b. 1949*

CHAMELEON

In your cosmic repose
only the scandal
of two rolling planets betrays your avid
flypaper soul.
Wrapped in technicolour, worked
by fastidious
shifting-spanner toes,
each foot is
lifted slowly
one by
one by one, painstaking
on the track
of flies.

Pinnacle-back, confuser of nature's
metaphysical divides
on the ground evoking
your volcanic beginnings
you become
a stone among stones.
Or you climb up
into the arms of a tree and the tree
blushes
it thinks it has grown a strange
insectivorous leaf.
Last of the fire-breathers,
tongue-in-cheek dragon with your secret
mouthful of rolled-up pink
I have seen you
finally old with age
tiptoe to the end
turn a deep brown and wear
your own death
like another disguise.

Patrick Cullinan *South Africa, b. 1932*

THE FIRST, FAR BEAT
from ESCARPMENT

In the mountains
the first, far beat
of Spring thunder:

thick with young,
a lizard on the rock
moves its head

and in the flank
the quick heart pulses.

D H Lawrence *UK, 1885–1930*

LIZARD

A lizard ran out on a rock and looked up, listening
no doubt to the sounding of the spheres.
And what a dandy fellow! the right toss of a chin for you
and swirl of a tail!

If men were as much men as lizards are lizards
they'd be worth looking at.

Biblically, a 'leviathan' is a sea-monster. Be sure to note the change of subject in the second stanza: it is now the lizard that is referred to.

Douglas Livingstone *South Africa, b. 1932*

LEVIATHAN

A puff-adder, khaki,
fatter than a stocking of pus
except for its short thin tail,
obese and quick
as certain light-footed dancers
took a dozing lizard.

Scaly little monster
with delicate hands and feet
stupidly sluggish in the sun.
Panting, true,
but lizards breathe mostly
as if their lives depended.

Gone.
Enveloped by a slack
wormy yellow bowel.

O Jonah, to tumble to
those sickly deadly depths,
slick walled, implacably black.

VELD AND VLEI POEM

Up from the vlei, over the veld,
a herdboy trots for the kopje,
bare feet thudding on tufts,
soles sensory, cold-shouldering thorns;
head down, breaks into full pelt
—bare skin starting to tremble—
up the small hill for vantage,
hand over hand over ledges;
linked by flickering tongues of lightning
silent thunderheads assemble.

A blunted Ace-of-Spades head
big as a terrier's stills;
a sensory tongue flickers;
coils etched in fresh geometry,
faded harlequin's hammock-skin shed,
the fat viper crams the tense juncture
of a narrow ledge and its overhang;
hinged on skeletal levers, fangs
of slender wet porcelain wait
spring-loaded for puncture.

THE KING

Old Tawny's mane is moth-
eaten now, a balding monk's tonsure,
and his fluid thigh muscles flop
slack as an exhausted boxer's;

Creaks a little and is
just a fraction under fast (he's lame)
in those last short lethal rushes
at the slim white-eyed winging game;

Can catch them still of course,
the horny old claws combing crimson
from the velvet flanks in long scores,
here in the game-park's environs;

Each year, panting heavily,
manages with aged urbanity
to smile full-faced and yellowly
at a thousand box cameras.

Robert Graves *UK, 1895–1986*

FLYING CROOKED

The butterfly, a cabbage-white,
(His honest idiocy of flight)
Will never now, it is too late,
Master the art of flying straight,
Yet has—who knows so well as I?—
A just sense of how not to fly:
He lurches here and here by guess
And God and hope and hopelessness.
Even the aerobatic swift
Has not his flying-crooked gift.

Perseus Adams *South Africa, b. 1933*

BIRD SHRINE

'Look! Three tumblers, four croppers, two
fantails and a homer!' the boy
face aglow, illuminating his pigeon-hok
his treasure
as though it were an altar,
cast into shadow my teacher's inquiry
as to why he had been absent from school,
a place where he scored well below par,
and ushered me in to his house of snow.

Slowly, the joy in his eyes kindled mine;
I grew by degrees into the captured
height he saw, the weight those frail
arrowy bodies
lifted each time he came towards them.
Droughts, deserts were forgotten here,
the pain of being a failure on the curbed side
of the colour line; his alcoholic father.
With infinite care I rode the shaft

between his wonder and the wrapt gleams
of their attention, tasting the sky
the altitude in their blue-veined throbbing
                                        till I was baptized
and rebaptized in a spring of benediction.
Very gently, he drew out a fantail
handing it to me as if it were a white cloud.
Gratefully I received it, held it:
It crooned, a feathered hymn in my palms.

And he stood there then, no brown-skinned truant
child, but a connoisseur of diminutive
incandescent lives, a quick agent
                                        in a stratagem of light.
'Do you see? Do you see?' he asked. I did.
Quietly we returned to his beat-up shack,
I tutored, brimming with his sun-trade
and he–smiling, acting as if he'd ceded
me shares in his pure wealth–which he had.

Norman MacCaig *UK, b. 1910*

INTERRUPTION TO A JOURNEY

The hare we had run over
Bounced about the road
On the springing curve
Of its spine.

Cornfields breathed in the darkness,
We were going through the darkness and
The breathing cornfields from one
Important place to another.

We broke the hare's neck
And made that place, for a moment,
The most important place there was,
Where a bowstring was cut
And a bow broken forever
That had shot itself through so many
Darknesses and cornfields.

It was left in that landscape.
It left us in another.

Douglas Livingstone *South Africa, b. 1932*

GENTLING A WILDCAT

Not much wild life, roared Mine leonine Host
from the fringe of a forest of crackles
round an old dome-headed steam radio,
between hotel and river—a mile of bush—
except for the wildcats and jackals.

And he, of these parts for years, was right.
That evening I ventured with no trepidations
and a torch, towed by the faculty
I cannot understand, that has got me
into too many situations.

Under a tree, in filtered moonlight,
a ragged heap of dusty leaves stopped moving.
A cat lay there, open from chin to loins;
lower viscera missing; truncated tubes
and bitten-off things protruding.

Little blood there was, but a mess of
damaged lungs; straining to hold its breath
for quiet; claws fixed curved and jutting,
jammed open in a stench of jackal meat;
it tried to raise its head hating the mystery, death.

The big spade-skull with its lynx-fat cheeks
aggressive still, raging eyes hooked in me, game;
nostrils pulling at a tight mask of anger
and fear; then I remembered hearing
they are quite impossible to tame.

Closely, in a bowl of unmoving roots,
an untouched carcass, unlicked, swaddled and wrapped
in trappings of birth, the first of a litter stretched.
Rooted out in mid-confinement: a time
when jackals have courage enough for a wildcat.

In some things too, I am a coward,
and could not here punch down with braced thumb,
lift the nullifying stone or stiff-edged hand
to axe with mercy the nape of her spine.
Besides, I convinced myself, she was numb.

And oppressively, something felt wrong:
not her approaching melting with earth,
but in lifetimes of claws, kaleidoscopes:
moon-claws, sun-claws, teeth after death,
certainly both at mating and birth.

So I sat and gentled her with my hand,
not moving much but saying things, using my voice;
and she became gentle, affording herself
the influent luxury of breathing–
untrammelled, bubbly, safe in its noise.

Later, calmed, despite her tides of pain,
she let me ease her claws, the ends of the battle,
pulling off the trapped and rancid flesh.
Her miniature limbs of iron relaxed.
She died with hardly a rattle.

I placed her peaceful ungrinning corpse
and that of her firstborn in the topgallants
of a young tree, out of ground reach, to grow: restart
a cycle of maybe something more pastoral
commencing with beetles, then maggots, then ants.

Musaemura Zimunya *Zimbabwe, b. 1949*

CATTLE IN THE RAIN

Nothing has no end,
it is true.
This rain used to soak us in the pastures
and the cattle would not stop to graze,
they would not be driven to the kraal,
it made me cry and curse sometimes
and I used to wish I was born for the skirt.
Just imagine penetrating the wet bush
almost doubled up
with a heavy smelling coned up jute sack
as a rain coat,
pebbles of water pounding on the head,
very irritating, too.
Sometimes an angry wasp disturbed by the foregoing
cows
stabbed you on the cursing lips
and in the frantic stampede,
wet thorns snapped at random in your benumbed feet.
And the rain does not cease
and the cows just go on.

Come to the kraal–
This ox, called Gatooma,
stands still before the rest,
his ghost of silent disapproval shattering to your mind,
listening, listening to nothing at all,
and I knew then that I had to call for help.
But people at home in warm huts
could hardly hear me through the maddening rain.
This ox, tail high,
at two sniffs and a cajole,
all meant to humiliate
would crash through the thin bush
leaving me running weakly
sobbing at each step

a bone of anger blocking my breath,
chugging after the rhythmic hooves hammering the
  earth.
and still it rained
and the cows went skelter
and the rain swept the salty tears
and watery mucus into my lips.

Denise Levertov *USA, b. 1923*

THE RAINWALKERS

An old man whose black face
shines golden-brown as wet pebbles
under the streetlamp, is walking
two mongrel dogs of dis-
proportionate size, in the rain,
in the relaxed early-evening avenue.

The small sleek one wants to stop,
docile to the imploring soul of the trashbasket,
but the young tall curly one
wants to walk on; the glistening sidewalk
entices him to arcane happenings.

Increasing rain. The old bareheaded man
smiles and grumbles to himself.
The lights change: the avenue's
endless nave echoes notes of
liturgical red. He drifts

between his dogs' desires.
The three of them are enveloped—
turning now to go crosstown—in their
sense of each other, of pleasure,
of weather, of corners,
of leisurely tensions between them
and private silence.

"Not everyone thinks – or is – the same"

Lionel Abrahams *South Africa, b. 1928*

THE WHITEMAN BLUES

Two cars, three loos, a swimming pool,
Investment paintings, kids at a private school . . .
we entertain with shows or gourmet food–
and yet we don't feel right, we don't feel good.

Why doesn't the having help?
Why doesn't the spending save?
Why doesn't the fun–
Why doesn't the culture–
Why don't the ads add up to something?

We can afford to say we know
the blacks are really given hell,
Big Boss is harsh and stupid and must go:
we say it–and it helps like one Aspro.
We still feel jumpy, mixed up, not quite well.

Which specialist can cure the thing we've got–
the got-it, gotta-get-it blues,
the deep-freeze, cheaper wholesale, world excursion blues?
We're high on the know-all-about-it booze.
We're bursting with kwashiorkor of the bank.
We're depressed by the whiteman blues.

In the backyards they pray for us.
In Soweto they see our plight.
In the border areas they understand.
In the Bantustans they wait
to pat our shoulder, hold our hand.
They know, they know,
to them it isn't news:
we've got these lost-man, late-man,
money-man, superman,
whiteman blues.

Dannie Abse *UK, b. 1923*

RED BALLOON

It sailed across the startled town,
over chapels, over chimney-pots,
wind-blown above a block of flats
before it floated down.

Oddly, it landed where I stood,
and finding's keeping, as you know.
I breathed on it, I polished it,
till it shone like living blood.

It was my shame, it was my joy,
it brought me notoriety.
From all of Wales the rude boys came,
it ceased to be a toy.

I heard the girls of Cardiff sigh
when my balloon, my red balloon,
soared higher like a happiness
towards the dark blue sky.

Nine months since, have I boasted of
my unique, my only precious;
but to no one dare I show it now
however long they swear their love.

'It's a Jew's balloon,' my best friend cried,
'stained with our dear Lord's blood.'
'That I'm a Jew is true,' I said,
said I, 'that cannot be denied.'

'What relevance?' I asked surprised,
'what's religion to do with this?'
'Your red balloon's a Jew's balloon,
let's get it circumcized.'

Then some boys laughed and some boys cursed,
some unsheathed their dirty knives:
some lunged, some clawed at my balloon,
but still it would not burst.

They bled my nose, they cut my eye,
half conscious in the street I heard,
'Give up, give up your red balloon.'
I don't know exactly why.

Father, bolt the door, turn the key,
lest those sad, brash boys return
to insult my faith and steal
my red balloon from me.

Charles Mungoshi *Zimbabwe, b. 1947*

CHRISTMAS

Here is neon bright First Street:
a kaylite feast of imitation fir trees
slow-sledge-pulling reindeer
silent feather-weight bells
under sweltering southern stars.

And here I am; born to fear the lion
abhor the vulture, turn back
on seeing a squirrel crossing my path
cipher dark meanings from
the otter's droppings
ward off the potent of the owl's hoot
with amulets and roots.

Here I am; impotent in the middle
of all this bloodless white magic—
Could this be the Messiah?
(I came but you would not remember me?)
Even the eldest of my ancestors
don't know what snow looks like.

Richard Rive *South Africa, b. 1931*

WHERE THE RAINBOW ENDS

Where the rainbow ends,
There's going to be a place, brother,
Where the world can sing all sorts of songs,
And we're going to sing together, brother,
You and I,
Though you're White and I'm not.
It's going to be a sad song, brother,
'Cause we don't know the tune,
And it's a difficult tune to learn,
But we can learn it, brother,
You and I,
There's no such tune as a Black tune,
There's no such tune as a White tune,
There's only music, brother,
And it's the music we're going to sing,
Where the rainbow ends.

Sipho Sepamla *South Africa, b. 1932*

FEELING SMALL

They can take me
on a predawn ride
to an 8 a.m. hearing
they can cram me
into a people's coach
to ride
to their splendid offices
they can call me
boy
even as a retired pensioner
they can give me a yearly rise
and take it as fast as c.o.l.
I say they can move me

from slums
to a peachtree-lined Location
to squat temporarily
they can kick me
in the arse
just to ask me to shift a bit
they can be solemn
explaining the justness of their duty
protecting me from skelms and so on
I say they can beat their breasts
a thousand, thousand times
to show
how they've made God listen at times
to rationalizations
But brother!
they can never, never be so large hearted
to free themselves of fear
'Strue's living God!

Adam Small *South Africa, b. 1936*

O KROESKOP!

Bushy head
so they call you
to insult you
bushy head
but bushy head
birds can nest in you
daily fly from you
and return to you
carrying home to you
in their wings for you
heaven;
have their young in you
hold their young in you

till they fly from you
and return to you
carrying home to you
in their wings for you
heaven

bushy head
so they call you
to insult you
bushy head
but bushy head
you can accommodate
heaven

Patrick Cullinan *South Africa, b. 1932*

THE BEACH, EVENING

And now the tide's way out, the sun just hot
And a wide buck nigger in blue jeans walks
The open sand. The whites glare. Black. It's not
Just colour, it's his stance. He preens, he stalks.

All his body swings with nerve, with pounds
Of insolence. Slap into the waves
He bounces, fully clad. And this astounds
No one. He leaps and waves his arms. He saves

Nothing. Emerges dripping, shining. Rapist!
Faker! Hopped up, slapping wet, he doubles
On the spot: then does a backward twist.
An exercise that no one sees, troubles

To see. He lopes off. Disappears. And on
The pink horizon a yacht comes up, met
By stares and teatime. All day has gone.
And now: red sails. The bloody sunset.

Wole Soyinka *Nigeria, b. 1934*

TELEPHONE CONVERSATION

The price seemed reasonable, location
Indifferent. The landlady swore she lived
Off premises. Nothing remained
But self-confession. 'Madam,' I warned,
'I hate a wasted journey–I am African.'
Silence. Silenced transmission of
Pressurized good-breeding. Voice, when it came,
Lipstick coated, long gold-rolled
Cigarette-holder pipped. Caught I was, foully.
'HOW DARK?' . . . I had not misheard . . . 'ARE YOU LIGHT
OR VERY DARK?' Button B. Button A. Stench
Of rancid breath of public hide-and-speak.
Red booth. Red pillar-box. Red double-tiered
Omnibus squelching tar. It *was* real! Shamed
by ill-mannered silence, surrender
Pushed dumbfoundment to beg simplification.
Considerate she was, varying the emphasis–
'ARE YOU DARK? OR VERY LIGHT?' Revelation came.
'You mean–like plain or milk chocolate?'
Her assent was clinical, crushing in its light
Impersonality. Rapidly, wave-length adjusted,
I chose. 'West African sepia'–and as afterthought,
'Down in my passport.' Silence for spectroscopic
Flight of fancy, till truthfulness clanged her accent
Hard on the mouthpiece. 'WHAT'S THAT?' conceding
'DON'T KNOW WHAT THAT IS.' 'Like brunette.'
'THAT'S DARK, ISN'T IT?' 'Not altogether.
Facially, I am brunette, but madam, you should see
The rest of me. Palm of my hand, soles of my feet
Are a peroxide blonde. Friction, caused–
Foolishly madam–by sitting down, has turned
My bottom raven black–One moment madam!'–sensing
Her receiver rearing on the thunderclap
About my ears–'Madam,' I pleaded, 'wouldn't you rather
See for yourself?'

Chris Zithulele Mann *South Africa, b. 1948*

TO LUCKY WITH HIS GUITAR ON A GRAHAMSTOWN STREET

Here comes Lucky, the tallest of the tall;
born in P E; raised on a farm; not young
(nineteen); hardly been to school (no money);
can't find a job (no schooling); clouds of
brisk-eyed sparrows perch inside his guitar.

So here's Lucky, Coolhand Lucky the Tall;
Sunday afternoon; easing into town;
hasn't a word (drifting over New Street);
nothing to tell us (tapping the pavement);
but Coolhand riffs; zig-zag bass; stringshine chords.

And here's a car; a Chevvy; it's slowing,
it's parking. Nope. The missus is waving.
She's scared. Nope, she's angry; she has something
to say, yes, she's rolling down the window.
Lady? 'What are you kaffirs doing in town?'

Silence; the tar's wet; a truck bakes and ticks.
For Christ's sake, say something! You're the tallest,
Lucky, give it to her! Stupid old bitch.
Here it comes . . . Nope. Coolhand won't stop riffing.
The notes fly up like sparrows (for today).

Don Mattera *South Africa, b. 1935*

FOR A CENT

Each morning
Corner of pritchard and joubert,
Leaning on a greasy crutch
Near a pavement dustbin
An old man begs
Not expecting much.

His spectacles are cracked and dirty
He does not see my black hand
Drop a warm cent into his scurvy palm
But instinctively he mutters:
        Thank you my Baas!

Strange
        That for a cent
        A man can call his brother, BAAS!

Shabbir Banoobhai *South Africa, b. 1949*

HE'S A GOOD BOY, THIS ONE

he's a good boy, this one
i don't know what we'd do
without him
he knows where everything is
all the prices
the regular customers' likes and dislikes
and he's only been here a year

yes, he is a good man
this boy
who's never heard
about being your brother's keeper
and turning the other cheek
but still manages to smile
as baas
leans on the crutch of his shoulder
as he stumbles to a chair
in the sun
then shrugs him off
as if he were swatting an irritating fly

Dylan Thomas *UK, 1914–1953*

THE HUNCHBACK IN THE PARK

The hunchback in the park
A solitary mister
Propped between trees and water
From the opening of the garden lock
That lets the trees and water enter
Until the Sunday sombre bell at dark

Eating bread from a newspaper
Drinking water from the chained cup
That the children filled with gravel
In the fountain basin where I sailed my ship
Slept at night in a dog kennel
But nobody chained him up.

Like the park birds he came early
Like the water he sat down
And Mister they called Hey mister
The truant boys from the town
Running when he had heard them clearly
On out of sound

Past lake and rockery
Laughing when he shook his paper
Hunchbacked in mockery
Through the loud zoo of the willow groves
Dodging the park keeper
With his stick that picked up leaves.

And the old dog sleeper
Alone between nurses and swans
While the boys among willows
Made the tigers jump out of their eyes
To roar on the rockery stones
And the groves were blue with sailors

Made all day until bell time
A woman figure without fault
Straight as a young elm
Straight and tall from his crooked bones
That she might stand in the night
After the locks and chains

All night in the unmade park
After the railings and shrubberies
The birds the grass the trees the lake
And the wild boys innocent as strawberries
Had followed the hunchback
To his kennel in the dark.

Brian Patten *UK, b. 1946*

PARK NOTE

Disgusted by the weight of his own sorrow
I saw one evening
a stranger open wide his coat
and taking out from under it his heart
throw the thing away.

Away over the railings, out across the parks,
across the lakes and the grasses,
as if after much confusion
he had decided not to care but

to move on lightly, carelessly,
amazed and with a grin upon his face
that seemed to say, 'Absurd
how easy that was done.'

Daniel Hoffman *USA, b. 19—*

THE CENTER OF ATTENTION

As grit swirls in the wind the word spreads.
On pavement approaching the bridge a crowd
Springs up like mushrooms.
They are hushed at first, intently

Looking. At the top of the pylon
The target of their gaze leans toward them.
The sky sobs
With the sirens of disaster crews

Careening toward the crowd with nets,
Ladders, resuscitation gear, their First
Aid attendants antiseptic in white duck.
The police, strapped into their holsters,

Exert themselves in crowd-control. They can't
Control the situation.
Atop the pylon there's a man who threatens
Violence. He shouts, *I'm gonna jump–*

And from the river of upturned faces
–Construction workers pausing in their construction work,
Shoppers diverted from their shopping,
The idlers relishing this diversion

In the vacuity of their day–arises
A chorus of cries–*Jump!*
Jump! and *No–*
Come down! Come down! Maybe, if he can hear them,

They seem to be saying *Jump down!* The truth is,
The crowd cannot make up its mind.
This is a tough decision. The man beside me
Reaches into his lunchbox and lets him have it,

Jump! before he bites his sandwich,
While next to him a young blonde clutches

Her handbag to her breasts and moans
Don't *Don't* *Don't* so very softly

You'd think she was afraid of being heard.
The will of the people is divided.
Up there he hasn't made his mind up either.
He has climbed and climbed on spikes imbedded in the pylon

To get where he has arrived at.
Is he sure now that this is where he was going?
He looks down one way into the river.
He looks down the other way into the people.

He seems to be looking for something
Or for somebody in particular.
Is there anyone here who is that person
Or can give him what it is that he needs?

From the back of a firetruck a ladder teeters.
Inching along, up, up up up up, a policeman
Holds on with one hand, sliding it on ahead of him.
In the other, outstretched, a pack of cigarettes.

Soon the man will decide between
The creature comfort of one more smoke
And surcease from being a creature.
Meanwhile the crowd calls *Jump!* and calls *Come down!*

Now, his cassock billowing in the bulges of Death's black flag,
A priest creeps up the ladder too.
What will the priest and the policeman together
Persuade the man to do?

He has turned his back to them.
He has turned away from everyone.
His solitariness is nearly complete.
He is alone with his decision.

No one on the ground or halfway into the sky can know
The hugeness of the emptiness that surrounds him.
All of his senses are orphans.
His ribs are cold andirons.

Does he regret his rejection of furtive pills,
Of closet noose or engine idling in closed garage?
A body will plummet through shrieking air,
The audience dumb with horror, the spattered street . . .

The world he has left is as small as toys at his feet.
Where he stands, though nearer the sun, the wind is chill.
He clutches his arms—a caress, or is he trying
Merely to warm himself with his arms?

The people below, their necks are beginning to ache.
They are getting impatient for this diversion
To come to some conclusion. The priest
Inches further narrowly up the ladder.

The center of everybody's attention
For some reason has lit up a butt. He sits down.
He looks down on the people gathered, and sprinkles
Some of his ashes upon them.

Before he is halfway down
The crowd is half-dispersed.
It was his aloneness that clutched them together.
They were spellbound by his despair

And now each rung brings him nearer,
Nearer to their condition
Which is not sufficiently interesting
To detain them from business or idleness either,

Or is too close to a despair
They do not dare
Exhibit before a crowd
Or admit to themselves they share.

Now the police are taking notes
On clipboards, filling the forms.
He looks round as though searching for what he came down for.
Traffic flows over the bridge.

Carl Sandburg *USA, 1878–1967*

ELEPHANTS ARE DIFFERENT TO DIFFERENT PEOPLE

Wilson and Pilcer and Snack stood before the zoo elephant.

Wilson said, 'What is its name? Is it from Asia or Africa? Who feeds it?
Is it a he or a she? How old is it? Do they have twins? How much does
it cost to feed? How much does it weigh? If it dies how much will another
one cost? If it dies what will they use the bones, the fat, and the hide for?
What use is it besides to look at?'

Pilcer didn't have any questions: he was murmuring to himself,
'It's a house by itself, walls and windows, the ears come from tall corn-
fields, by God; the architect of those legs was a workman, by God; he
stands like a bridge out across deep water; the face is sad and the eyes
are kind; I know elephants are good to babies.'

Snack looked up and down and at last said to himself, 'He's a tough son-of-a-gun outside and I'll bet he's got a strong heart, I'll bet he's strong as a copper-riveted boiler inside.'

They didn't put up any arguments.
They didn't throw anything in each other's faces.
Three men saw the elephant three ways
And let it go at that.
They didn't spoil a sunny Sunday afternoon;
'Sunday comes only once a week,' they told each other.

"It's a good feeling to be in love"

Michele Freind *South Africa, b. 1952*

busstop

i saw a nice boy
with long sideburns
and short hair and a blue suit.
he stood in front of me in the bus queue.

when the bus came
he stood back
to let me climb into the bus in front of him.

i turned to thank him
he gave me a radiant smile
it warmed my heart and made my day beautiful.

and then (wrapt in a haze of rosy dreams)
i tripped
and fell into the bus
flat on my stupid face.

Elizabeth Spilhaus *South Africa, b. 1950*

TO PHILIP

It seems just yesterday
when skies were blue,
I held your hand;
we walked along the beach—
the wind was cool;
I felt your body close;
then side by side
we soaked ourselves in sun.
Now all is gone:
I sit and sweat in school.
I know that somewhere
You are sweating too—
the difference is you have forgotten me
and oh, tall-Philip, how I think of you!

Douglas Livingstone *South Africa, b. 1932*

GIOVANNI JACOPO MEDITATES (ON UNISEX)

Vile, booby-trapping, little Crook!
Driving behind your Chestnut-Mane,
I thought you female, overtook
Your beaky Profile male & vain.

Adam Small *South Africa, b. 1936*

TIME SIGNAL
a ritual verse of the Cape

Noon thundering from Signal Hill
is a symbol
like the flashy array of the coons
is a symbol
like everything reckless like the South Easter
is a symbol
like the skolly's knife
is a symbol
like the herbs sold on the Parade
is a symbol
like the Malay man's crimson fez
is a symbol
like the Square with its flowers
is a symbol
like autumn in the Avenue
is a symbol
like everything, everything, like the Mountain itself
is a cymbal
taking the beating of our deeds
and reverberating loud and clear
like noon from Signal Hill
it's time
it's time to love!

Achmat Dangor *South Africa, b. 1948*

SCORN

They stopped us
outside the station,
'Where's your pass?
And you? Portuguese?
O! Malayer hê?
God. With a kaffir girl.'

I held you then,
Dear Ina, dear Ina,
flower of the night
wilting in the merciless light.

Be sure to speak *this poem, and much of its meaning will become clear. For instance: of = if; avarybudy = everybody; clearlink = the Afrikaans word 'Kleurling', a so-called Coloured person.*

Sipho Sepamla *South Africa, b. 1932*

DA SAME, DA SAME

I doesn't care of you black
I doesn't care of you white
I doesn't care of you India
I doesn't care of you clearlink
if sometimes you Saus Afrika
you gotta big terrible, terrible
somewheres in yourselves

I mean for sure now
all da peoples is make like God
an' da God I knows for sure
He make avarybudy wit' one heart

for sure now dis heart go-go da same
dats for meaning to say
one man no diflent to anader

so now
you see a big terrible terrible stand here
how one man make anader man feel
da pain he doesn't feel hisself
for sure now dats da whole point

sometime you wanna know how I meaning for
is simple
when da nail of say da t'orn tree
scratch little bit little bit of da skin
I doesn't care of say black
I doesn't care of say white
I doesn't care of say India
I doesn't care of say clearlink
I mean for sure da skin
only one t'ing come for sure
an' da one t'ing for sure is red blood
dats for sure da same, da same for avarybudy
so for sure now
you doesn't look anader man in de eye

Sipho Sepamla *South Africa, b. 1932*

A WISH

I have rivalled the birds in the air
enfolded by clouds even

I've been given to bend the sky at night

I am an atlas in my own right
holding back mighty rivers or changing their course

I defy distance reducing it to a point
as little as my hand

listen, I have pulled myself out of
the earth's warm womb glittering

I am that kind of man

but a wish of mine remains
peace at all times with all men

"Sometimes the place you're in makes a difference"

Shimmer Chinodya *Zimbabwe, b. 1957*

AFRICAN GRASS

Grass grows here, enough
To thatch a thousand roofs.
Tall khaki African grass
Two heads taller than I, laden
With beads of dew
In the early morning. Shove armfuls aside
To pass.

Grass caressing my bare thighs
Sweeping past me, rustling softly
like lovers.
Adam and Eve once walked here
Naked and innocent in this wild savannah;
When the world was young
And there was no one else to watch.

It's hard to think that this tall crop
Coarse in its maturity
Burst out of October's black burnt plains
Green and succulent, and savouring the mellow sun
Green to this height.
  But it's harder yet to think
That this crop will crumple
To veld fire ashes;
Fruitless growth!

This whispering
Shall be
Gone.

Patrick Cullinan *South Africa, b. 1932*

ON THE WILD COAST

On the wild coast the cattle
come down to the sea after grazing.
They lie in the sand together, staring:
the sea comes in and goes out.

They walk away at the cool
of evening, slow to the top
of the dunes then bellow and kick
down the other side homewards

for milking: and darker
they move through the smoke and they stop
at the houses. The voices
are loud and then soft;

women talking to children,
the murmur of men at the fires.

Jeni Couzyn *South Africa, b. 1942*

IN THE HOUSE OF THE FATHER

Christmas, the turning time, the final reckoning and the
forgiveness, we rode towards each year, over humps of
bitterness, towards the father

omnipotent and bountiful night rider with his magical
reindeer and sack full of gifts—
you could rely on him always to be there when you got there

accept the culmination of your year in his lap
hear all, forgive with a wish, and let you
begin all over;

a time of reprieve and new resolutions, time when you could
believe in new beginnings, a time of peace and long
playtime. With a hand in the dark

it began before dawn. The sun would rise over the city
as we passed the last gold hills of the mine dumps. Always
I saw children leaping up them, and in my head, in golden depths

a heap of little skeletons. Then the long hot hours dreaming
through the dorps each its single tree and tin roofs blazing
each its lone dog barking and black silent men

propped on the verandah of the general store, drinking
lemonade. Endless car games, the singing game chanting every
    rhyme we knew
from ten green bottles to jesus loves me over the veld

to pass the time. At last, crossing, purple and lonely
the valley of a thousand hills, the tropical
deep smell of heavy flowers would glut the evening

and my father offered sixpence for the first to see the sea.
And there it was after a sudden unbending–that immense blue
    promise.
Then inland into the sugar cane in the deep of night

the rustle of dunes and the sugar cane fields
the farmers who kept pythons fifty feet long to keep the rats down
and at midnight

the cottage. O the damp smell of foliage, smell of salt
and the sea's heavy breathing in the night, stray cries
of live things; batswing, shadow, sleep, and a ring of mornings.

The snakes were the price. In their hundreds they inhabited
our world at christmas. They were the hazard
in the garden. And they were everywhere

tangled in undergrowth, slithering over your feet in the pathway
stretched across doorways in the sun
lurking under the banana plant and nesting in the luckybean tree

they were everywhere, everywhere. And happiness was
    everywhere
in the father's time, who came down from heaven
in his red dressing gown and my father's shoes at the appointed
    time

cottonwool beard lopsided across his grin
his arms full of parcels.
His was the future that always came, keeping its promise.

In the house of the father the year would turn
a flower full blown, shedding its petals.
Glistened in your hand a free gift, a clean seed.

Patrick Cullinan *South Africa, b. 1932*

MADAGASCAR
For Chris and Lee Hope

I am walking by the sea,
The sun is hot enough:
It warms the sand,
The wind blows along.

A black man is fishing
From a rock. The fish
At his feet are dead.
Today is not different.

A bamboo stem
Is running gripped by
A dog's jaw. The legs
Are moving.

Nothing is said as things
Are done. This is
The natural way
Things go on.

Two butterflies before me
Fly up and down.
They are gold or red.
Two or three steps
Then the wind takes them;
They drift in air and light
Toward the surf.
  It is clear
They'll never make it
To Madagascar.

Musaemura Zimunya *Zimbabwe, b. 1949*

MY HOME

I live in the highlands
encompassed by great green ridges
where is my home,
in the heart of the storms of the world?
Is this my home?
Brother, it is;
also beats with
the whole of Africa's pulse
conveying day into darkness
and darkness into sunshine.

Upon those storms and billows of mountains
capped with the surf of transient mists,
whale-like woolly objects slumber
crowns of bulky trees sway
and tilt, tilt
and sway
in the grace of breathing breezes.

And now I can see
the silver glare and glisten
of the full sliding sun
in a huge serpent
like a river clear of muddy flood

flowing and leaping swift and free
gurgling and giggling
like those rude young girls from the city
gurgling and giggling
swayed by mini-morals
clothing the old chaste tradition
with everlasting defilement.

Never mind sister
this is our home
houses full of smoke
and pendent soot
full of the odour of life
you see those umbrellas of tawny grass thatch
piping dark blue wreaths of smoke
from rowdy beer-fires?
They shelter our people
poor in clothes and heart
moonshine cheerful in eyes and lips
and us too.

Sipho Sepamla *South Africa, b. 1932*

ADRIAANSPOORT

Down there below
where I can see no spoor
of man or animal
there is a winding
of what used to be
there is a swaying
of lanky tufts of grass
there is a meandering
of leafy protea trees
there is an ageing
of variegated pelindaba rocks
and there is a thought
of dead spirits
once clashing by day
only to retreat at sunset
leaving these parts wild at night
yet serene under the moon

where I stand
there is no stench with which to live
only the giddy smell of braaied boerewors
already the plastic plates are full of stywe mielie-pap
a table is laden with sliced cheese and green salads
for amidst the chattering of adults in French
and the fooling around of our children in no
language of words
we are going to revel
beyond the mischievous hand of man

there is a spirit moving where we are
we turn faces to avoid it
hardly being successful
for we are part of the being of things

there are clouds gathering above our heads
we say it will not rain
hardly being correct
for the earth needs to be swept at times

it rains! . . . pula! . . . it rains! . . . pula!

Sydney Clouts *South Africa, 1926–1982*

FIREBOWL

Kalahari Bushman fires flowing
in the hollows of the desert
click all night
stick stuck upright
click
click
of starlight
bowstring
toes of the eland
thk thk the big raindrops
tk tk tk the sandgrains
drinking.
Sssskla!
sparks of honey
arrowheads
we who dance
around the circle
around the circle
spoor him
find him

my arrow clings to the thick thick
grunt of darkness
my arrow sings through fire

we who dance we find
the
fire
of the fire.

C J Driver *South Africa, b. 1939*

WHITE RIVER, TRANSVAAL

In my home country
The trees burn, the tall grass burns.
Soon they'll burn the hill my name's on,
All that shaped the ground,
Tree and grass, stone and water,
Burn, will burn.

Arthur Nortje *South Africa, 1942–1970*

AT LANSDOWNE BRIDGE

After the whoosh of doors slid shut
at Lansdowne Bridge I swim in echoes.
Who fouled the wall O people?
FREE THE DETAINEES someone wrote there.

Black letters large as life stare you
hard by day in the black face;
above the kikuyu grass to the sandflats
goes the boorish clang-clang of railways.

Darkness neutralizes the request
till dawn falls golden and sweet,
though a sudden truck by night
cornering, holds it in spidery light.

Jennifer Davids *South Africa, b. 1945*

LOCATION FIRES

Beneath my eyelids
the landscape is heavy
the people are buried in ground-
clinging shapes of houses

From Langa to Nyanga
the fires are hidden
the landscape is flattened
frightened and silenced

Where are the fires
for me to believe in
where are the tongues of flame
to lick and conquer the dark

In answer the black body
of the sky rears up
loud with roaring
voices of the stars

The stars tonight
are blue backyard fires
studding the black
location of the sky

Achmat Dangor *South Africa, b. 1948*

PARADISE

Oh paradise,
cool paradise of Africa
your sea roars
like the restless roots
of our lives

and yet does not give life
to the dreams
of the people
you have forgotten.

Here, around me,
they destroy my city.
District Six,
they dismantle you
–stone by stone
rock of my history.

On the walls
of my last refuge
cockroaches run
secretive and quiet,
an omen:
love and hope
that will have to
be hidden in darkness.

Somewhere in the twilight
a banjo trills, somewhere
on an overgrown terrace
people sing and people laugh,
the human voices of everyday.

Oh paradise, cool paradise
of Africa,
what memories you recreate.

Oh why, why do you
tighten the chains?

C J Driver *South Africa, b. 1939*

IN CHAPEL STREET

In Chapel Street there's a cross
High on Calvary Hill
Where a man is crucified. The gloss
Of his paint has faded

And royal Christ hangs naked, come rain
Or shine. No token
For that god but a broken body
And the silent mouths

Of his side and hands. Do you see
Religion in that man
Hangs there? I stand where I see
A testament of pain

In his postures of agony. No more.
But the priest in my blood
Worships till the head's high laws
Totter. But not fall.

There were too many lies that were told
And promises broken
And holier vows than mine forgotten. But that old
As his hill Christ

Dies hard, though his fisherman heart
Nets nothing but lies
And fallacies. There is no part
Of him that does not move me.

In Chapel Street there are no lies
Of religion can touch
The christ hangs high over the city, eyes
And hands perpetually still.

"There're some interesting people around"

Efficacy = 'producing the desired effect'. When pronouncing it, the stress is on the first syllable: ef**fi**cacy*, not on the second:* ef*fi*cacy*.*

Casey Motsisi *South Africa, 1932–1977*

THE EFFICACY OF PRAYER

They called him Dan the Drunk.
The old people refuse to say how old he was,
Nobody knows where he came from – but they all
Called him Dan the Drunk.
He was a drunk, but perhaps his name was not really Dan.
Who knows, he might have been Sam.
But why bother, he's dead, poor Dan.
Gave him a pauper's funeral, they did.
Just dumped him into a hole to rest in eternal drunkenness.
Somehow the old people are glad that Dan the Drunk is dead.
Ghastly!
They say he was a bad influence on the children.
But the kids are sad that Dan the Drunk is no more.
No more will the kids frolic to the music that used to flow out of his battered concertina. Or listen to the tales he used to tell.
All followed him into that pauper's hole.
How the kids used to worship Dan the Drunk!
He was just one of them grown older too soon.
'I'm going to be just like Dan the Drunk,' a little girl said to her parents of a night cold while they crowded around a sleepy brazier.
The parents looked at each other and their eyes prayed.
'God Almighty, save our little Sally.'
God heard their prayer.
He saved their Sally.
Prayer. It can work miracles.
Sally grew up to become a nanny. . . .

Fhazel Johennesse *South Africa, b. 1956*

THE NIGHTWATCHMAN

the fire looks warm from here
and a red reflection diffuses and
glows across his face
he sits quite still a grey overcoat
drawn taut over his back
then i see his fingers move   agitate
and briefly a flicker of firelight
paints a smile on his face and then
melts it again
i watch his fingers   they slowly
slip across the scalloped edge
of the knobkerrie
and suddenly i know

i know that he waits for the
cracking of skulls and the
breaking of bones

Charles Causley *UK, b. 1917*

TIMOTHY WINTERS

Timothy Winters comes to school
With eyes as wide as a football-pool,
Ears like bombs and teeth like splinters:
A blitz of a boy is Timothy Winters.

His belly is white, his neck is dark,
And his hair is an exclamation-mark.
His clothes are enough to scare a crow
And through his britches the blue winds blow.

When teacher talks he won't hear a word
And he shoots down dead the arithmetic-bird,
He licks the patterns off his plate
And he's not even heard of the Welfare State.

Timothy Winters has bloody feet
And he lives in a house on Suez Street,
He sleeps in a sack on the kitchen floor
And they say there aren't boys like him any more.

Old Man Winters likes his beer
And his missus ran off with a bombardier,
Grandma sits in the grate with a gin
And Timothy's dosed with an aspirin.

The Welfare Worker lies awake
But the law's as tricky as a ten-foot snake,
So Timothy Winters drinks his cup
And slowly goes on growing up.

At Morning Prayers the Headmaster helves
For children less fortunate than ourselves,
And the loudest response in the room is when
Timothy Winters roars 'Amen!'

So come one angel, come on ten:
Timothy Winters says 'Amen
Amen amen amen amen.'
Timothy Winters, Lord.
Amen.

Roger McGough *UK, b. 1937*

MY BUSCONDUCTOR

My busconductor tells me
he only has one kidney
and that may soon go on strike
through overwork.
Each busticket
takes on now a different shape
and texture.
He holds a ninepenny single
as if it were a rose
and puts the shilling in his bag
as a child into a gasmeter.
His thin lips
have no quips
for fat factorygirls
and he ignores
the drunk who snores
and the oldman who talks to himself
and gets off at the wrong stop.
He goes gently to the bedroom
of the bus
to collect
and watch familiar shops and pubs passby
(perhaps for the last time?)
The sameold streets look different now
more distinct
as through new glasses.
And the sky
was it ever so blue?

And all the time
deepdown in the deserted busshelter of his mind
he thinks about his journey nearly done.
One day he'll clock on and never clock off
or clock off and never clock on.

Lawrence Ferlinghetti *USA, b. 1919*

IN GOLDEN GATE PARK THAT DAY

In Golden Gate Park that day
a man and his wife were coming along
thru the enormous meadow
which was the meadow of the world
He was wearing green suspenders
and carrying an old beat-up flute
in one hand
while his wife had a bunch of grapes
which she kept handing out
individually
to various squirrels
as if each
were a little joke

And then the two of them came on
thru the enormous meadow
which was the meadow of the world
and then
at a very still spot where the trees dreamed
and seemed to have been waiting thru all time
for them
they sat down together on the grass
without looking at each other
and ate oranges
without looking at each other
and put the peels
in a basket which they seemed
to have brought for that purpose
without looking at each other

And then
he took his shirt and undershirt off
but kept his hat on
sideways
and without saying anything

fell asleep under it
And his wife just sat there looking
at the birds which flew about
calling to each other
in the stilly air
as if they were questioning existence
or trying to recall something forgotten

But then finally
she too lay down flat
and just lay there looking up
at nothing
yet fingering the old flute
which nobody played
and finally looking over
at him
without any particular expression
except a certain awful look
of terrible depression

Chris Zithulele Mann *South Africa, b. 1948*

IN PRAISE OF THE SHADES

Hitching across a dusty plain last June,
down one of those deadstraight platteland roads,
I met a man with rolled-up khaki sleeves,
who told me his faults, and then his beliefs.
It's amazing, some people discuss more
with hitchhikers than even their friends.

His bakkie rattled a lot on the ruts,
so I'm not exactly sure what he said.
Anyway, when he'd talked about his church,
and when the world had changed from mealie-stalks
to sunflowers, which still looked green and firm,
he lowered his voice, and spoke about his shades.

This meant respect I think, not secrecy.
He said he'd always asked them to guide him,
and that, even in the city, they did.
He seemed to me a gentle balanced man,
and I was sorry to stick my kitbag
onto the road again and say goodbye.

When you are alone and brooding deeply,
do all your teachers and loved ones desert you?
Stand on a road when the fence is whistling.
You say, 'It's the wind', and if the dust swirls,
'Wind again', although you never see it.
The shades work like the wind, invisibly.

And they have always been our companions,
dressed in the flesh of the children they reared,
gossiping away from the books they left,
a throng who even in the strongest light
are whispering, 'You are not what you are,
remember us, then try to understand'.

They come like pilgrims from the hazy seas
which shimmer at the borders of a dream,
not such spirits that they can't be scolded,
not such mortals that they can be profaned,
for scolding them, we honour each other,
and honouring them, we perceive ourselves.

When all I ever hear about these days
is violence, injustice, and despair,
or worse than that, humourless theories
to rescue us all from our human plight,
those moments in a bakkie on a plain
make sunflowers from a waterless world.

e e cummings *USA, 1894–1962*

BUFFALO BILL'S

Buffalo Bill's
defunct
who used to
ride a watersmooth-silver
stallion
and break onetwothreefourfive pigeonsjustlikethat
Jesus

he was a handsome man
and what i want to know is
how do you like your blueeyed boy
Mister Death

"You get one helluva fright"

Christopher Cheek *UK, b. 1946*

ACCIDENT

Ahh! at last, nearly five-thirty.
Now just the long leisurely cleaning of the bacon machine
All keen, I'll grease the wheel.
One bit of odd fat and round and round like french polishing
Gently to the blade, no blood, no pain, how neat
But off again as quick as lightning.
Go to the office
Interrupt manager–sacrilege.
'O.K. son I'm a St John's man you know'–pompous to the last.

Masses of blood now,
Still no pain–cheated.
'Sorry about the blood on your floor'–crawl to the last.
Now the reward–the shop girls
'Oh my poor dear–does it hurt?'
Wince
'Well you know'
Wince again
'Only a little'
Oh boy! great–
Perhaps a scar to talk about
Shivering with excitement.
'Come on son I'll give you a lift to the hospital.'

The title of the next poem is taken from Shakespeare's Macbeth. *In thinking about living and dying, Macbeth uses this image:*

> *Out, out, brief candle. Life's but a walking shadow . . .*

And he goes on to make some other very interesting comparisons. See if you can find the reference in the last Act of the play.

Robert Frost *USA, 1875–1964*

'OUT, OUT – '

The buzz saw snarled and rattled in the yard
And made dust and dropped stove-length sticks of wood,
Sweet-scented stuff when the breeze drew across it.
And from there those that lifted eyes could count
Five mountain ranges one behind the other
Under the sunset far into Vermont.
And the saw snarled and rattled, snarled and rattled,
As it ran light, or had to bear a load.
And nothing happened: day was all but done.
Call it a day, I wish they might have said
To please the boy by giving him the half hour
That a boy counts so much when saved from work.
His sister stood beside them in her apron
To tell them 'Supper'. At the word, the saw,
As if to prove saws knew what supper meant,
Leaped out at the boy's hand, or seemed to leap–
He must have given the hand. However it was,
Neither refused the meeting. But the hand!
The boy's first outcry was a rueful laugh,
As he swung toward them holding up the hand
Half in appeal, but half as if to keep
The life from spilling. Then the boy saw all–
Since he was old enough to know, big boy
Doing a man's work, though a child at heart–
He saw all spoiled. 'Don't let him cut my hand off–
The doctor, when he comes. Don't let him, sister!'
So. But the hand was gone already.
The doctor put him in the dark of ether.
He lay and puffed his lips out with his breath.
And then–the watcher at his pulse took fright.
No one believed. They listened at his heart.
Little–less–nothing! –and that ended it.
No more to build on there. And they, since they
Were not the one dead, turned to their affairs.

Modikwe Dikobe *South Africa, b. 1913*

A NIGHT HAWK

Straddled on ding-tong bell bicycle
Is a blue-nine
A Blue-sky jail-breaker
On Harley-Davidson handlebars
        Reed-swaying.

On shiny bicycle
Ding-tong bells
Reed-swaying
To lavish on my sister's earnings
This ragamuffin
Blue-sky five-star prisoner.

A Blue-sky blue-nine
Unreformed parole
Reed-swaying on dong-tong bicycle
        Reconnoitring.

Five-star Blue-sky blue-nine
Unrepented criminal
Undeterred
Skips over the fence.

A night hawk
Experienced burglar
No second to waste
Thins into the night.

'Morena!
What is this?'
A five-star Blue-sky blue-nine
Passionately moved
By baby in arms
Retraces his way
        'I am sorry, madam.'

Fhazel Johennesse *South Africa, b. 1956*

THE NIGHT TRAIN

there is no comfort here
in this third class coach
on this green resisting seat
i twitch and glance around –
there are few too few travellers
on the night train
crossing my legs and flicking
my cigarette i turn to stare
through the window
into the darkness outside
(or is it my reflection i stare at)
and glance impatiently at the wrong
stations we stop at
out
i must get out of here soon
for in this coach there is a smell
which haunts me
not the smell of stale man but
the whispering nagging smell of fear

Mutiswayo Shandu *South Africa*

BYE BYE, OVERCOAT

The day before yesterday Mr Straun
gives me this overcoat. Today I catch
this train to my Stepmother's, wearing it.
It is a splendid coat, fawn, almost new
– just this small gap in the seam of one sleeve.

It is past midday, the train not crowded
with mostly shoppers and halfday meisies.
Still, I am standing, straphanging, swaying
but I prefer it: such a cool garment
of such swaggering cut should not be creased.

Comes payday: a good hat – maybe a fine
snapbrim fedora, perhaps from PATEL'S
is quite definitely indicated.
Stepmama has a Singer at her place . . .
The air around me goes into deepfreeze.

Turning, I see at the far end: Main Ou
has joined us, accompanied by a pair
of toughlooking tsotsis. Over dozens
of heads his eyes meet mine. He is staring
at my new overcoat.Tixo! Such luck!

They start working the silent, sullen folks,
towards me: peering in wallets, purses,
emptying handbags; some men have to stand
to have their back-pockets patted. Main Ou
does not work or hang on. His legs are braced.

He hardly moves with the train's rock and roll.
He taps a bicyclespoke with a stained
wood handle, coolly, on his left thumbnail.
His two thugs work quietly and quickly:
it is nearly all money and trinkets . . .

But one man has already lost his fine
leather jacket. Bruce Lee, where are you now!
There are dozens of us, just three of them.
As usual, each of us is alone
against the predator, the oppressor . . .

For once, even the SAP would do!
When I reach Stepmama's distinctive house
I am too sad to speak, and she sees it.
She serves me tea, strokes my defeated neck.
Her Singer stays, unused, under her bed.

A kwela = the colloquial term for a police pick-up van, from the Zulu verb 'to climb in'. Dompas = the colloquial name for the pass or reference book that all black South Africans until very recently had to carry with them all the time. (See also the two poems that follow this one.)

Mafika Gwala *South Africa, b. 1946*

KWELA RIDE

Dompas!
I looked back
Dompas!
I went through my pockets
Not there.

They bit into my flesh (handcuffs).

Came the kwela-kwela
We crawled in.
The young men sang.
In that dark moment

It all became familiar.

Note in the following poem that Mono is the poet's wife.

Stan Motjuwadi *South Africa, b. 1926*

TAKEN FOR A RIDE

I get my cue
from the glint in the cop's eye.
I have seen it before.
So I have to find it.

I pull away from Mono
and hug myself in desperation.
Up, down, back, front, sides,
like a crazed tribal dancer.
I have to find it.

Without it I'm lost, with it I'm lost,
a cipher in Albert Street.
I hate it. I nurse it,
my pass, my everything.

Up, down, back, front, sides,
Mono's lip twitches,
She looks at me with all the love.
She shakes her head nervously.
Up, front, sides, back, down,
like a crazed tribal dancer.
Molimo!

The doors of the kwela-kwela gape,
I jabber at Mono.
The doors swing lazy, sadistic like Jonah's whale.
I take a free ride.

James Matthews *South Africa, b. 1929*

THE FACE OF MY MOTHER TAKES THE SHAPE

the face of my mother takes the shape of
a frightened mouse
at the sound of a policeman's step
the fear-filled flutter of her heart
a bird ensnared
my father freezes his feelings at the demand
for a pass
and i watch the fire in his
eyes slowly die
as his hands grope for the right to survive

The poem that follows was written at the time of the Soweto '76 disturbances (see p. 3).

Sipho Sepamla *South Africa, b. 1932*

I SAW THIS MORNING

I saw this morning
panic in the location
little children clasping schoolbags
put to flight
I saw them run across an open veld
up and down the streets
they were seeking the refuge of their homes
I saw terror whirl around and about the
location
little children fleeing from an unseen monster
I heard the screams of a child
he was a crippled little boy
yelling
tears furrowing his cheeks
he was wheeling around his teacher
held tight
no words reached him
no bullying cowed him
his mind was gripped by this fear

I saw this morning
what it is like
to be scared by rumour

Edwin Morgan *U K, b. 1920*

GLASGOW 5 MARCH 1971

With a ragged diamond
of shattered plate-glass
a young man and his girl
are falling backwards into a shop-window.
The young man's face
is bristling with fragments of glass
and the girl's leg has caught
on the broken window
and spurts arterial blood
over her wet-look white coat.
Their arms are starfished out
braced for impact,
their faces show surprise, shock,
and the beginning of pain.
The two youths who have pushed them
are about to complete the operation
reaching into the window
to loot what they can smartly.
Their faces show no expression.
It is a sharp clear night
in Sauchiehall Street.
In the background two drivers
keep their eyes on the road.

Damian Ruth *South Africa, b. 1954*

BEZUIDENHOUT

We rose.
The orderly pulled him to his feet.
The judge had said
'no extenuating circumstances' and 'no alternative'.
The sentence was read.
The boy's eyes sped
from judge to orderly

to his mother
in the gallery.

His brother had taken his bicycle
without his permission.
He had run down the dusty location road,
and stabbed him dead.

Now his body was jerking.
The orderly closed in.
The judge left the court
quite white in the face.
It had taken him two days
to understand the story
because they were country coloureds
and spoke Afrikaans differently
and witnesses contradicted each other.

His mother
leant over the gallery
and asked 'Wat makeer?'
The orderly walked past,
drew his finger across his throat,
and said, 'Hy kry die tou.'

She rose,
silent and slowly it seemed,
her arms reaching out
in tattered coat sleeves,
threw her head back and screamed
NEE, NEE, HY'S MY KIND, MY LAASTE KIND.
EK HET NIE MEER KINDERS NIE!
Her husband stopped twisting his hat
and dragged her out the court.

I used her words to start my newspaper report.
But now, eight years later, when I remember it,
I think above all of
not a terrified jerking face
not a scarecrow mother crucified
but of the orderly, Bezuidenhout,
dragging his finger across his own throat.

Philip Larkin *UK, 1922–1986*

DAYS

What are days for?
Days are where we live.
They come, they wake us
Time and time over.
They are to be happy in:
Where can we live but days?
Ah, solving that question
Brings the priest and the doctor
In their long coats
Running over the fields.

Lenrie Peters *Gambia, b. 1932*

PARACHUTE MEN

Parachute Men say
The first jump
Takes the breath away
Feet in the air disturbs
Till you get used to it.

Solid ground
Is not where you left it
As you plunge down
Perhaps head first
As you listen to
Your arteries talking
You learn to sustain hope

Suddenly you are only
Holding an open umbrella
In a windy place
As the warm earth
Reaches out to you
Reassures you
The vibrating interim is over

You try to land
Where the green grass yields
And carry your pack
Across the fields.

The violent arrival
Puts out the joint
Earth has nowhere to go
You are at the starting point

Jumping across worlds
In condensed time
After the awkward fall
We are always at the starting point.

“Being a kid was fun . . .”

Sylvia Plath *USA and UK, 1932–1963*

The poet's daughter Frieda was conceived in America, and born in England on 1 April 1961. *See also the poem Frieda's father, Ted Hughes, wrote about her, p. 16.*

YOU'RE

Clownlike, happiest on your hands,
Feet to the stars, and moon-skulled,
Gilled like a fish. A common-sense
Thumbs-down on the dodo's mode.
Wrapped up in yourself like a spool,
Trawling your dark as owls do.
Mute as a turnip from the Fourth
of July to All Fools' Day,
O high-riser, my little loaf.

Vague as fog and looked for like mail.
Farther off than Australia.
Bent-backed Atlas, our traveled prawn.
Snug as a bud and at home
Like a sprat in a pickle jug.
A creel of eels, all ripples.
Jumpy as a Mexican bean.
Right, like a well-done sum.
A clean slate, with your own face on.

D H Lawrence *UK, 1885–1930*

BABY RUNNING BAREFOOT

When the white feet of the baby beat across the grass
The little white feet nod like white flowers in a wind,
They poise and run like puffs of wind that pass
Over water where the weeds are thinned.

And the sight of their white playing in the grass
Is winsome as a robin's song, so fluttering;
Or like two butterflies that settle on a glass
Cup for a moment, soft little wing-beats uttering.

And I wish that the baby would tack across here to me
Like a wind-shadow running on a pond, so she could stand
With two little bare white feet upon my knee
And I could feel her feet in either hand

Cool as syringa buds in morning hours,
Or firm and silken as young peony flowers.

Shimmer Chinodya *Zimbabwe, b. 1957*

RECOLLECTION

I remember this wood only too well.
I remember these crouching thorn trees (– it seems
they've hardly grown ever since I last saw them –)
And these criss-crossing bush paths
Bordering a coarse crop of grass yellowed
With the dust stirred up
By swishing feet of children, and
The wind of course.
I remember too, the chirping of the timid little birds.

I remember how we used to run barefoot
Under these thorn trees.
Three brothers with feet full of thorns –
Bird-shooting we were, with rough made little catapults

That exploded into our own faces.
And pockets full of jingling stones picked up somewhere.
Between us we shot down one bird in a year.

I remember the big sign that said
Something about people not being allowed in –
And we, heedless, half ignorant prowlers
Made the wood our hunting-ground
And birds and bitter little berries our prey.

I remember it only too well . . .
I remember even more now, how young we were then
And how this scrub bush
Growing patched and ungreen – a short walk
From the township's street of grim houses
Satisfied our boyish dreams.

Leslie Pickett *UK, b. 1946*

THE ONE THAT GOT AWAY

Don't talk to me about the one
That got away. You should
'Ave seen wot 'appened.
There I was, sitting there wiv me
Rod in one 'and, and a sammidge
In the uvver, minding me own
Business and then it 'appened.
Me old reel started flying round and
Me old rod bent over and then
Ping!
The bloody lot 'ad gone.
All me line 'ad gone orf me
Reel and me rod was still shaking
From the vibrashun w'en me line went
And me rod flicked back.
I was flabbergasted! I just sat
There wiv 'alf a sammidge in me
'And, and me mouf wide open.

In the next poem, a staffrider = one who gets a ride on a train, usually (and often very dangerously) on the outside of it.

Motshile Nthodi *South Africa, b. 1948*

STAFFRIDER

Black boy
no recreation centre
no playing grounds
no money for lunch at school
not enough schoolbooks
No proper education
no money for school journeys

but
one Saturday morning
my father gave me
one shilling and six pennies
he said
my son
go and make enough
for a living

With eleven pennies
I bought a return ticket to town
the remaining seven for provision
good enough

I was one of those
carry-boys at the municipal market
caddy at the golf course
selling oranges and peanuts
illegally on the trains

money money money
that's not enough for a boy
what about entertainment

right
I am seventeen by now
waiting on a station platform
waiting for the conductor's
whistle of command
waiting for the train
to roll on its permanent rail

now steel wheels of an electric train
start playing a tune of
percussion and trombone
from the middle of the platform
pulling myself from the crowd
waiting for the tube to the north

like a bebop dancer
I turn around twice
and I open the window
push up the frame with my elbow
grab the frame between
the window and the door

listen to the improvisation
from my dirty oversize
canvas shoes
pha – – phapha – phapha –
pha – phapha – phapha –
phapha – phapha –

listen to the shouting
and whistles
from the audience in that tube
when I swing on the outer handle
and rest on the bottom stair

THAT'S THEATRE HEY

they see me once
but only once
I'm on top of the coach
lying eight inches under
the main power lines

ACROBATIC HEY

they see me once again
but only once
I'm under the coach
lying on a steel frame
next to the wheels

CIRCUS HEY

fifteen stations
stupids packed
sardines in the tube
phapha – pha –
poor black eyes on me
– phapha –
home station
– pha – phapha – phaphaphaphapha

WA SALA WENA

– phaphapha –
railway police chasing me
I jump the platform
the railway line
the fence
across the river
towards home
I'm safe

this is the Saturday programme
and till we meet again
thank you brothers and sisters,
thank you.

D H Lawrence *UK, 1885–1930*

PIANO

Softly, in the dusk, a woman is singing to me;
Taking me back down the vista of years, till I see
A child sitting under the piano, in the boom of the tingling strings
And pressing the small, poised feet of a mother who smiles as she sings.

In spite of myself, the insidious mastery of song
Betrays me back, till the heart of me weeps to belong
To the old Sunday evenings at home, with winter outside
And hymns in the cosy parlour, the tinkling piano our guide.

So now it is vain for the singer to burst into clamour
With the great black piano appassionato. The glamour
Of childish days is upon me, my manhood is cast
Down in the flood of remembrance, I weep like a child for the past.

"... Not for everyone, though"

D H Lawrence *UK, 1885–1930*

DISCORD IN CHILDHOOD

Outside the house an ash-tree hung its terrible whips,
And at night when the wind rose, the lash of the tree
Shrieked and slashed the wind, as a ship's
Weird rigging in a storm shrieks hideously.

Within the house two voices arose, a slender lash
Whistling she-delirious rage, and the dreadful sound
Of a male thong booming and bruising, until it had drowned
The other voice in a silence of blood, 'neath the noise of the ash.

Mafika Gwala *South Africa, b. 1946*

ONE SMALL BOY LONGS FOR SUMMER
(for Bill Naughton)

The kettle hisses
Mother moves about the kitchen
sliding from corner to corner.
The fire from the stove
pierces into the marrow.
And mother pushing towards the stove
warns of the steam.
My young brother, Thamu, jerks my arm
violently: Stop leaning on me, your elbow
has sunk into my thigh.
            Apology
                    I wasn't aware.

The kettle sings
            Some distant far-away song?
Mother picks it up
with an almost tender care.
Sets me thinking of a war-picture
The actor carefully setting the charge
and smiling all the time

I'll also be a soldier
when I'm old – why, Uncle Shoba was one.
Father drops the paper on the table
He comes to join us
– staring coldly round.
It's no frown really,
But he's grinding his jaws.
Maybe it's the July
Handicap.

The kettle purrs now
Steam is escaping; it kisses the ceiling
and vanishes. Mother is pouring the violent waters
into the coffee-jug. Coffee.
Yes, I need some coffee – a mug of hot coffee.
Very rousing.
We can't play outside – I must not go, I know
How we danced in the rain. We are so tired
of the winter: It's so dingy outside.
We can't play inside – I'm so tied up.
It's so boring, I feel like bursting into
a cracking laughter; but father,
he'll go mad.
It's so steamy inside
I feel I could bite the walls down.
If only it makes the winter pass.

Countee Cullen *USA, 1903–1946*

INCIDENT

Once riding in old Baltimore
Heart-filled, head-filled with glee,
I saw a Baltimorean
Keep looking straight at me.

Now I was eight and very small,
And he was no whit bigger,
And so I smiled, but he poked out
His tongue, and called me, 'Nigger'.

I saw the whole of Baltimore
From May until December;
Of all the things that happened there
That's all that I remember.

Sydney Clouts *South Africa, 1926–1982*

ROY KLOOF

'Such a little king's eye', said my mother
who still had the kind imperial look.
'He'll command. Dear cherry-bright boy!'
Her faded English blood ran strong,
she dreamt of the shires all night long,
rose in the morning and called me, Roy.

That was the beginning. My father who came
raw from the veld with a rocky name,
though a mild man, frequently dreamt
that Circumstance galloped with him riding,
that History was thatched into his roof.
It hurt him to hear me christened, Roy Kloof.

Up behind father with little bright spurs
I dreamt I was galloping, gravely horsed.
I dreamt of a sceptre; I cried and I cried
till rock and shire were divorced.
Division incarnate! An unhappy role!
My country has given me flint for a soul.

Fhazel Johennesse *South Africa, b. 1956*

EXTRA

swivelling on the corner
the paper waving in the air
like a rag on a washline
his anxious whistle low
cupped between his hoarse cries
his beseeching
compelling demand that you buy
the paper
his striped skipper
awkward pants
heeled tackies
his angry ebony skin
his bangle that spins on his wrist
and his desolate humility
that he should sell
news of a life
that always
passes him by

Mbuyiseni Oswald Mtshali *South Africa, b. 1940*

BOY ON A SWING

Slowly he moves
to and fro, to and fro,
then faster and faster
he swishes up and down.

His blue shirt
billows in the breeze
like a tattered kite.

The world whirls by:
east becomes west,
north turns to south;
the four cardinal points
meet in his head.

Mother!
Where did I come from?
When will I wear long trousers?
Why was my father jailed?

Alan Paton *South Africa, b. 1903*

DANCING BOY

Small boy I remember you
I remember you used to dance here
By the roadside
And the white people stopped in their cars
And when you had finished dancing
Gave money to you.

Sir, I am the one indeed
I remember you stopped in your car
And when I had finished dancing
Gave money to me.

Small boy you are the one indeed
But why are you not dancing?
Do you not dance here any more?

Sir, I do not dance here any more
For one day when I was dancing
A white man stopped here in his car
And he came at me trembling
Like nothing I had seen before
And he thrust money at me
Great piles of paper money
Into my very hands and cried
For God's sake and for Christ's sake
Do not dance here any more.

I took this money to my father
And he said to me
It's a deep thing and a dark thing
And I do not understand it
But you must not dance there any more.

Sir, that is why
Although I am the one indeed
I do not dance here any more.

Concerning the title of the next poem . . . The first part of the word, 'ptera–' is the Greek for 'wing', and the word is often used in describing prehistoric animals. Does that information help? Perhaps a friendly biologist will explain.

Douglas Livingstone *South Africa, b. 1932*

PTERANODON

A seven year old herd boy,
ragged happy and vacant,
sits alone playing the stonegame,
his back to the five
thin healthy head grazing.

Across the valley
the distant warts of huts
squat on the wrist of the hill.

Long believed extinct,
there was no one
but the walleyed
stampeding clot of cattle
to see the two dozen
feet of dusty leather
wingspread, hear the wet
crush of long toothed jaws closing,
the snap of vertebrae,
and nothing, nothing at all
the flight away
with the broken rabbit boy
one limb slow waving.

"Some of the people you meet . . ."

Mongane Serote *South Africa, b. 1944*

BEERHALL QUEEN

Her arm V-folded within the tin
That's clenched under her armpit,
She strides, her gait straight,
Her bare feet slide fast,
Her eyes fixed far
She nears the beerhall.
On her way back
She's the Queen;
She's slow in her strides
Careful in her holds –
That are as tender now as a mother's hand –
Round the tin that's on her head
Bubbling the bitter brown beer
That keeps men and husbands
Away from this troublous world,
Together in her warm homely house.

Musaemura Zimunya *Zimbabwe, b. 1949*

OLD GRANNY

A little freezing Spider
Legs and arms gathered in her chest
Rocking with flu,
I saw old Granny
at Harare Market;
It was past nine of the night
When I saw the dusty crumpled Spider –
A torn little blanket
Was her web.

Jeremy Cronin *South Africa, b. 1949*

IN BLUE BLUER-THAN-ANY-SEA DOEKS

In blue bluer-than-any-sea doeks, in rubber galoshes,
Arm over arm, three lunch-time pals,
Three dark women and their laughter

As opposite the cannery my train arrives
From many years back and
Slows into Woodstock station.

Three women eating lunch, glimpsed
From the window.
Salt light for laughter, galoshes
Studded with a cat's
Eyed blink in a myriad of pellicles.

Three women, six knowing hands
Fresh from, x the number,
Bodies of fishes.
In gutting and scaling there being, I'd guess,
No malice, nor any your equals.

Your hands planing cross-grain to the flesh,
Your galoshes collecting the soft milt
Spray of hake scales.
Into your tender propitious hands, sisters,
From the night parts of the seas, I commend
Lucky – all fishes.

Edwin Morgan *UK, b. 1920*

GOOD FRIDAY

Three o'clock. The bus lurches
round into the sun. 'D's this go—'
he flops beside me—'right along Bath Street?
—Oh tha's, tha's all right, see I've
got to get some Easter eggs for the kiddies.
I've had a wee drink, ye understand—
ye'll maybe think it's a—funny day
to be celebrating—well, no, but ye see
I wasny working, and I like to celebrate
when I'm no working—I don't say it's right
I'm no saying it's right, ye understand—ye understand?
But anyway tha's the way I look at it—
I'm no boring you, eh? —ye see today,
take today, I don't know what today's in aid of,
whether Christ was—crucified or was he—
rose fae the dead like, see what I mean?
You're an educatit man, you can tell me—
—Aye, well. There ye are. It's been seen
time and again, the working man
has nae education, he jist canny—jist
hasny got it, know what I mean,
he's jist bliddy ignorant—Christ aye,
bliddy ignorant. Well—' The bus brakes violently,
he lunges for the stair, swings down—off,
into the sun for his Easter eggs,
on very
          nearly
                    steady
                              legs.

Bernard Levinson *South Africa, b. 1926*

ELSIE

Elsie talked to God from her flat in Hillbrow.
Perched on the edge of her bath
she discussed the price of bread
and the things the butcher said
when she couldn't decide.

She was always grateful that He found her.
Between the Swop-shop and the Coffee bar
one could miss the door –
the metal steps to the fourth floor
and the dark corner
where the refuse drain rumbled and coughed.

The sun falls amongst chimneys
splinters in a million windows –
Are you there Elsie?
Are you there in the darkness –
in your own secret care
holding the remains of the day in a shopping bag?
Are you talking to God?

Shelley Swade *South Africa, b. 1952*

HEY, BEGGAR

Hey, beggar,
Old tattered man,
Sing with the wolves
To the moon
And the grain.

Laugh, old beggar,
With the wind
In your cheek
And the sound
Of the sea
In your shell.

Cold, beggar,
Freeze with the tree
In the snow,
Fringe your beard
With the frost
Of your bed.

And hey, beggar,
With the sun
In your eye
And a tooth
In the earth.

Sandy beggar,
Heaving the hay,
Be buried
With your body
Whole.

"So who's free?"

Chris van Wyk *South Africa, b. 1957*

INJUSTICE

Me, I cry easily if you're hurt
and I would've carried the crosses
of both the murderer
and the thief
if they'd've let me
and I'd've lived then.

I grasp helplessly at cigarettes
during riots
and burn my fingers
hoping.

My nose has never sniffed teargas
but I weep all the same
and my heart hurts
aching from buckshot.

My dreams these days are policed
by a million eyes
that baton-charge my sleep
and frog-march me into a
shaken morning.

I can't get used to injustice.
I can't smile no matter what.

I'll never get used to nightmares
but often I dream of freedom.

James Matthews *South Africa, b. 1929*

TRIP TO BOTSWANA

I had a taste
of freedom
the first cautious sip
causing
an unexperienced delight of
senses
my soul outpaced the girded
wings
transporting me from forced
confinement
my soul welcomed my
arrival
it stilled my trembling
flesh
as a woman and man
embraced though their colours were in
contrast
no hostile hand ripped them
apart
love blossoming on their
faces
my eyes became an eager
spectator
to the manifestations of
freedom
where within my captivity i was
denied
filled with the fruit of
freedom
my return holds no
fear
of the horror of my
slaughterhouse

Don Mattera *South Africa, b. 1935*

REMEMBER

Remember to call at my grave
When freedom finally
Walks the land
So that I may rise
To tread familiar paths
To see broken chains
Fallen prejudice
Forgotten injury
Pardoned pains.

And when my eyes have filled their sight
Do not run away for fright
If I crumble to dust again

It will only be the bliss
Of a long-awaited dream
That bids me rest
When freedom finally walks the land . . .

Zulu Molefe *South Africa*

BLACK ZIONIST MEETING

All the unsung poets
of this religion
all those who swear undying
loyalty with jehovah
are present tonight

'What will we say
on the cross?'
thunders the bearded preacher
as he leads his flock
like Moses out
    of the house of bondage

to meet jehovah
in prayer and song

For a few hours
        they
            are
                free.

Jorge Rebelo *Mozambique, b. 1940*

POEM

Come, brother, and tell me your life
come, show me the marks of revolt
   which the enemy left on your body

Come, say to me 'Here
my hands have been crushed
because they defended
the land which they own'

'Here my body was tortured
because it refused to bend
to invaders'

'Here my mouth was wounded
because it dared to sing
my people's freedom'

Come brother and tell me your life,
come relate me the dreams of revolt
which you and your fathers and forefathers
dreamed
in silence
through shadowless nights made for love

Come tell me these dreams become
war,
the birth of heroes,
land reconquered,
mothers who, fearless,
send their sons to fight.

Come, tell me all this, my brother.
And later I will forge simple words
which even the children can understand
words which will enter every house
like the wind
and fall like red hot embers
on our people's souls.

In our land
Bullets are beginning to flower.

Elizabeth Bishop *USA, 1911–1979*

THE BURGLAR OF BABYLON

On the fair green hills of Rio
  There grows a fearful stain:
The poor who come to Rio
  And can't go home again.

On the hills a million people,
  A million sparrows, nest,
Like a confused migration
  That's had to light and rest,

Building its nests, or houses,
  Out of nothing at all, or air.
You'd think a breath would end them,
  They perch so lightly there.

But they cling and spread like lichen,
   And the people come and come.
There's one hill called the Chicken,
   And one called Catacomb;

There's the hill of Kerosene,
   And the hill of the Skeleton,
The hill of Astonishment,
   And the hill of Babylon.

Micuçú was a burglar and killer,
   An enemy of society.
He had escaped three times
   From the worst penitentiary.

They don't know how many he murdered
   (Though they say he never raped),
And he wounded two policemen
   This last time he escaped.

They said, 'He'll go to his auntie,
   Who raised him like a son.
She has a little drink shop
   On the hill of Babylon.'

He did go straight to his auntie,
   And he drank a final beer.
He told her, 'The soldiers are coming,
   And I've got to disappear.

'Ninety years they gave me.
   Who wants to live that long?
I'll settle for ninety hours,
   On the hill of Babylon.

'Don't tell anyone you saw me.
   I'll run as long as I can.
You were good to me, and I love you,
   But I'm a doomed man.'

Going out, he met a *mulata*
   Carrying water on her head.
'If you say you saw me, daughter,
   You're just as good as dead.'

There are caves up there, and hideouts,
   And an old fort, falling down.
They used to watch for Frenchmen
   From the hill of Babylon.

Below him was the ocean.
   It reached far up the sky,
Flat as a wall, and on it
   Were freighters passing by,

Or climbing the wall, and climbing
   Till each looked like a fly,
And then fell over and vanished;
   And he knew he was going to die.

He could hear the goats *baa-baa*-ing,
   He could hear the babies cry;
Fluttering kites strained upward;
   And he knew he was going to die.

A buzzard flapped so near him
   He could see its naked neck.
He waved his arms and shouted,
   'Not yet, my son, not yet!'

An Army helicopter
   Came nosing around and in.
He could see two men inside it,
   But they never spotted him.

The soldiers were all over,
   On all sides of the hill,
And right against the skyline
   A row of them, small and still.

Children peeked out of windows.
  And men in the drink shop swore,
And spat a little *cachaça*
  At the light cracks in the floor.

But the soldiers were nervous, even
  With tommy guns in hand,
And one of them, in a panic,
  Shot the officer in command.

He hit him in three places;
  The other shots went wild.
The soldier had hysterics
  And sobbed like a little child.

The dying man said, 'Finish
  the job we came here for.'
He committed his soul to God
  And his sons to the Governor.

They ran and got a priest,
  And he died in hope of Heaven
—A man from Pernambuco.
  The youngest of eleven.

They wanted to stop the search,
  But the Army said, 'No, go on,'
So the soldiers swarmed again
  Up the hill of Babylon.

Rich people in apartments
  Watched through binoculars
As long as the daylight lasted.
  And all night, under the stars,

Micuçú hid in the grasses
  Or sat in a little tree,
Listening for sounds, and staring
  At the lighthouse out at sea.

And the lighthouse stared back at him,
  Till finally it was dawn.
He was soaked with dew, and hungry,
  On the hill of Babylon.

The yellow sun was ugly,
  Like a raw egg on a plate—
Slick from the sea. He cursed it,
  For he knew it sealed his fate.

He saw the long white beaches
  And people going to swim,
With towels and beach umbrellas,
  But the soldiers were after him.

Far, far below, the people
  Were little colored spots,
And the heads of those in swimming
  Were floating coconuts.

He heard the peanut vendor
  Go *peep-peep* on his whistle,
And the man that sells umbrellas
  Swinging his watchman's rattle.

Women with market baskets
  Stood on the corners and talked,
Then went on their way to market,
  Gazing up as they walked.

The rich with their binoculars
  Were back again, and many
Were standing on the rooftops,
  Among TV antennae.

It was early, eight or eight-thirty.
  He saw a soldier climb,
Looking right at him. He fired,
  And missed for the last time.

He could hear the soldier panting,
   Though he never got very near.
Micuçú dashed for shelter.
   But he got it, behind the ear.

He heard the babies crying
   Far, far away in his head,
And the mongrels barking and barking.
   Then Micuçú was dead.

He had a Taurus revolver,
   And just the clothes he had on,
With two contos in the pockets,
   On the hill of Babylon.

The police and the populace
   Heaved a sigh of relief,
But behind the counter his auntie
   Wiped her eyes in grief.

'We have always been respected.
   My shop is honest and clean.
I love him, but from a baby
   Micuçú was always mean.

'We have always been respected.
   His sister has a job.
Both of us gave him money.
   Why did he have to rob?

'I raised him to be honest,
   Even here, in Babylon slum.'
The customers had another,
   Looking serious and glum.

But one of them said to another,
   When he got outside the door,
'He wasn't much of a burglar,
   He got caught six times—or more.'

This morning the little soldiers
    Are on Babylon hill again;
Their gun barrels and helmets
    Shine in a gentle rain.

Micuçú is buried already.
    They're after another two,
But they say they aren't as dangerous
    As the poor Micuçú.

On the fair green hills of Rio
    There grows a fearful stain:
The poor who come to Rio
    And can't go home again.

There's the hill of Kerosene,
    And the hill of the Skeleton,
The hill of Astonishment,
    And the hill of Babylon.

Stanley Mogoba *South Africa*

TWO BUCKETS

A sleepy voice
from the confined space:
'Beware of the bucket
Move to the left;
        sleep there.
Any false move,
You fall into a lavatory bucket,
Or into drinking water next to it.'

In this startled manner,
I made my entry
Into a dark world,
Where thousands of men
Pine and are forgotten.

Hugh Lewin *South Africa, b. 1939*

BEHIND A BARRED WINDOW

Behind
  a barred window
    behind a high wall
watching
  a blood red
    Transvaal sun
rise
  brilliant through
    a distant bluegum
you fly
  high
    very high.

By way of introducing the next two poems: the poet's wife unexpectedly died while he was in prison.

Jeremy Cronin *South Africa, b. 1949*

VISITING ROOM

To admit light,
that's a window's vocation,
or a man to a wife
at this very place
where the wall becomes
for the briefest moments – a window,
shadowed by warders.
A glass plate, its sheer
quiddity, its coldness

forever between our hands.

I SAW YOUR MOTHER

I saw your mother
with two guards
through a glass plate
for one quarter hour
on the day that you died.

'Extra visit, special favour'
I was told, and warned
'The visit will be stopped
if politics is discussed.
Verstaan – understand!?'
on the day that you died.

I couldn't place
my arm around her,
around your mother
when she sobbed.

Fifteen minutes up
I was led
back to the workshop.
Your death, my wife,
one crime they managed
not to perpetrate
on the day that you died.

"What kind of world is this, then?"

D H Lawrence *UK, 1885–1930*

LET US BE MEN

For God's sake, let us be men
not monkeys minding machines
or sitting with our tails curled
while the machine amuses us, the radio or film or gramophone.

Monkeys with a bland grin on our faces.——

Alan Brownjohn *UK, b. 1931*

VITAL

I think my work is important, I am a link
In a long chain.
I had to have the training for it,
And I had to dirty my hands.
They ask my advice when they want to know
what would be best.
I might move up even higher, in time.

On Sunday, I woke up shouting. She said,
What on earth's the matter, we're supposed to be
Going out to dinner later; or rather lunch.
I dressed, and played with Lynda, and
Felt a bit better.

I was called into the office from the shop
Floor. 'Mr Fletton, up from London, wants to see you.'
But I was hearing the mutter-mutter,
The kind-of giggling noises inside the machines
Through four thick concrete walls.
I could not read the words in front of my eyes.

She said last Thursday, you haven't said a thing
The whole evening.
I said no. I've been watching.
. . . I couldn't name a thing I'd seen on the screen.

Today is vital, people are relying on me
To get ten thousand packages out on time.
I am part of a chain, a link, they ask my advice.
I open the front door. After the wind,
It's a lovely cool morning, and sun;
Very bright.
The keys of the Toledo are clenched wet
In my right hand. And I don't move.
I am standing shaking. I am standing, shaking.

Douglas Livingstone *South Africa, b. 1932*

TOWN TEMBU

This morning, the little missis smiled
at me, almost a man. Why?
She has not smiled at me for many months.
I do the two cars, the garden,
the floors, the windows, the swimming pool.
There are many empty bottles and full
ashtrays. Fat Agnes cooks,
washes, irons – one minute:
soft, pliant, touching; the next:
a touchy ringhals, which I prefer.
The boss drives off to work.
He drives back: a clock. Sometimes
he is drunk and walks in the garden. Then
we two become rare men together.

The madam drives the children to school,
drives back. She drinks coffee with friends
who come to talk, or talk of books
which they touch slowly like mysteries.
Her angers are strange puzzles: weeds,

broken plants, my times off.
The elder missis never looks at me.
I think we must hate each other.
The son is awful sometimes; sometimes
not bad. We swear at each other
with secret skill. When we are friends
he steals cigarettes which we smoke in my room.
In the past, the little missis always smiled.
She is growing, as I am.

I have picked up transparent things
from the floor, all over
the house: looked through them,
smelt them, some I have hugged
before putting them in the washbaskets.
I have a narrow bed, each leg
on two bricks for safety from the spirits.
I have a radio and friends who visit.
My mother says in two years
I can come home:
there are cattle, water, hills, a girl,
much ploughing – a man's work.
I am unsure. There is a factory
not far from here looking for men.

Sipho Sepamla *South Africa, b. 1932*

TO WHOM IT MAY CONCERN

Bearer
Bare of everything but particulars
Is a Bantu
the language of a people in southern Africa
He seeks to proceed from here to there
Please pass him on
Subject to these particulars
He lives
Subject to the provisions
Of the Urban Natives Act of 1925
Amended often
To update it to his sophistication
Subject to the provisions of the said Act
He may roam freely within a prescribed area
Free only from the anxiety of conscription
In terms of the Abolition of Passes Act
A latter-day amendment
In keeping with moon-age naming
Bearer's designation is Reference number 417181
And (he) acquires a niche in the said area
As a temporary sojourner
To which he must betake himself
At all times
When his services are dispensed with for the day
As a permanent measure of law and order
Please note
The remains of R/N 417181
Will be laid to rest in peace
On a plot
Set aside for Methodist Xhosas
A measure also adopted
At the express request of the Bantu
In anticipation of any faction fight
Before the Day of Judgement.

Paul Dehn *UK, b. 1912*

GUTTER PRESS

News Editor: Peer Confesses,
Bishop Undresses,
Torso Wrapped in Rug,
Girl Guide Throttled,
Baronet Bottled,
J.P. Goes to Jug.

But yesterday's story's
Old and hoary.
Never mind who got hurt.
No use grieving,
Let's get weaving.
What's the latest dirt?

Diplomat Spotted,
Scout Garrotted,
Thigh Discovered in Bog.
Wrecks Off Barmouth,
Sec in Yarmouth
Woman In Love With Dog,
Eminent Hostess Shoots Her Guests,
Harrogate Lovebird Builds Two Nests.

Cameraman: *Builds two nests?*
Shall I get a picture of the lovebird singing?
Shall I get a picture of her pretty little eggs?
Shall I get a picture of her babies?

News Editor: No!
Go and get a picture of her legs.

Beast Slays Beauty,
Priest Flays Cutie,
Cupboard Shows Tell-Tale Stain,
Mate Drugs Purser,
Dean Hugs Bursar,
Mayor Binds Wife with Chain,

Elderly Monkey Marries For Money,
Jilted Junky Says 'I Want My Honey'.

Cameraman: *'Want my honey?'*
Shall I get a picture of the pollen flying?
Shall I get a picture of the golden dust?
Shall I get a picture of a queen bee?

News Editor: No!
Go and get a picture of her bust.

Judge Gets Frisky,
Nun Drinks Whisky,
Baby Found Burnt in Cot,
Show Girl Beaten,
Duke Leaves Eton–

Cameraman: *Newspaper Man Gets Shot!*
May all things clean
And fresh and green
Have mercy upon your soul,
Consider yourself paid
By the hole my bullet made–

News Editor (dying): Come and get a picture of the hole.

John Betjeman *UK, 1906–1983*

EXECUTIVE

I am a young executive. No cuffs than mine are cleaner;
I have a Slimline briefcase and I use the firm's Cortina.
In every roadside hostelry from here to Burgess Hill
The *maitres d'hôtel* all know me well and let me sign the bill.

You ask me what it is I do. Well actually, you know,
I'm partly a liaison man and partly P.R.O.
Essentially I integrate the current export drive
And basically I'm viable from ten o'clock till five.

For vital off-the-record work—that's talking transport-wise—
I've a scarlet Aston-Martin—and does she go? She flies!
Pedestrians and dogs and cats—we mark them down for slaughter.
I also own a speed-boat which has never touched the water.

She's built of fibre-glass, of course. I call her 'Mandy Jane'
After a bird I used to know—No soda, please, just plain—
And how did I acquire her? Well to tell you about that
And to put you in the picture I must wear my other hat.

I do some mild developing. The sort of place I need
Is a quiet country market town that's rather run to seed.
A luncheon and a drink or two, a little *savoir faire*—
I fix the Planning Officer, the Town Clerk and the Mayor.

And if some preservationist attempts to interfere
A 'dangerous structure' notice from the Borough Engineer
Will settle any buildings that are standing in our way—
The modern style, sir, with respect, has really come to stay.

Wopko Jensma *South Africa, b. 1939*

OUR VILLAGE

since two gents with white suits rolled up
our village is not the same anymore

they pumped our chief full of bullets
they bumped off all our elders
they started raping our womenfolk
they keep talking of a new life for us
they say this thing is also elsewhere
they have our whole country tied up
they have come a long way to help us
they want us to have faith in them

our village is not the same anymore
since two gents with white suits rolled up

Musaemura Zimunya *Zimbabwe, b. 1949*

IFULAMACHINA (FLYING-MACHINE)

An old man
toddled in his field
his mind full of his hunger
full of fears of his precious seeds:
sons, and multiplying grandchildren.
Always thinking:
he had seen the ends of the cool first rains,
the end of zhizha![1]
of exploding green and milky cobs by the fireside
of harvests and festivals of millet beer
(weevils are beating drum skins under hovels)
he could reduce time
and count the years on his five fingers
everything else is coming to an end
people can still hold on, but not long
his thin self could think no more too.

Suddenly
it was thundering
and roaring everywhere
sand was vibrating
under the skin of the feet.

Slowly, surprised
like a semi-colon,
a bow-like hoe-handle
or like a spent murau[2] of the hunter
smoky twiggy spectacles hidden
in the deep sockets of the eye
one hand on the walking stick
another grasping the back
like that of the alert locust

he stopped
and mantis-like
slowly turned his head

uttered a soft laughter
a scrappy 'kee-kee-kee'
from his toothless infant mouth
his eyes fixed on a black trail of smoke
turning into clouds
in the hazy blue sky
pulled a fine long whistle
to fill his heart with this wonder
and in half empty voice
said, 'Ifulamachina',
following the trail of smoke
with his squinting eyes
and an innocent gumfull smile
until the black dot sunk behind the horizon,
'These men of the white skin,
even puffing into the face of God,
I swear through Chaminuka,[3]
they will finish us all off.'

---

[1] Luxuriant early summer

[2] Trap

[3] The Shona legendary hero who probably was warrior, magician, wiseman and many other things. Another explanation is that this figure was possibly a priest of the Mwari Cult.

D J Enright *UK, b. 1920*

TOURIST PROMOTION

For the tourists, who stay in the
Large new tourist hotels, the
Chief tourist attractions are the
Other large new tourist hotels.

For the querulous and wayward
There were once the local monkeys,
Who lived in the ancient tree-tops
Long before the hotels were thought of.

The tourists enticed the monkeys down
From the trees with monkey nuts and
Breakfast rolls. And the monkeys
Scampered across the road and were
Squashed by the buses transporting
Fresh tourists to see the monkeys.
It was not a pretty sight.

So now the tourists are confined to
The tourist hotels, large and new.
They pass with the greatest of ease
From one to the other, escorted by porters
With large new umbrellas, or even through
Underground passages, air-conditioned and
Adorned with murals by local artists,
Conveying impressions of the local scene.
After all, the tourist hotels were created
Specifically for the sake of the tourists.

Edwin Morgan *UK, b. 1920*

THE COMPUTER'S FIRST CHRISTMAS CARD

jollymerry
hollyberry
jollyberry
merryholly
happyjolly
jollyjelly
jellybelly
bellymerry
hollyheppy
jollyMolly
marryJerry
merryHarry
hoppyBarry
heppyJarry
boppyheppy

berryjorry
jorryjelly
moppyjelly
Mollymerry
Jerryjolly
bellyboppy
jorryhoppy
hollymoppy
Barrymerry
Jarryhappy
happyboppy
boppyjolly
jollymerry
merrymerry
merrymerry
merryChris
asmerryasa
Chrismerry
asMERRYCHR
YSANTHEMUM

William Plomer *South Africa, 1903–1973*

TO THE MOON AND BACK

countdown	takeoff
moonprints	rockbox
splashdown	claptrap

"Who lets this kind of thing happen?"

Vernon Scannell *UK, b. 1922*

BATTLEFIELDS

Tonight in the pub I talked with Ernie Jones
Who served with the Somersets in Normandy,
And we remembered how our fathers told
The sad and muddy legends of their war,
And how, as youngsters, we would grin and say:
'The old man's on his favourite topic now,
He never tires of telling us the tale.'
We are the old men now, our turn has come.
The names have changed–Tobruk and Alamein,
Arnhem, the Falaise Gap and Caen Canal
Displace the Dardanelles, Gallipoli,
Vimy Ridge, the Somme–but little else.
Our children do not want to hear about
The days when we were young and, sometimes, brave,
And who can blame them? Certainly not us.
We drank a last half pint and said goodnight.
And now, at home, the family is in bed,
The kitchen table littered with crashed planes;
A tank is tilted on its side, one track
Has been blown off; behind the butter-dish
Two Gunners kneel, whose gun has disappeared;
A Grenadier with busby and red coat
Mounts guard before a half a pound of cheese.
Some infantry with bayonets fixed begin
A slow advance towards the table edge.
Conscripted from another time and place
A wild Apache waves his tomahawk.
It's all a game. Upstairs, my youngest son
Roars like a little Stuka as he dives
Through dream, banks steep, then cuts his engine out,
Levels, re-enters the armistice of sleep.

D J Enright *UK, b. 1920*

STREETS

The poem was entitled 'The Streets of Hanoi',
It told of falling bombs and death and destruction
And misery and pain and wastage.
The poem was set to music, which told of death
And destruction and misery and pain and wastage.

A hall was found to play it in, a singer to sing it,
An orchestra to accompany the singer, and a printer
To print the programme . . . Whereupon it was felt
(Things being what they happened to be) that
The song had better be called 'The Streets of Saigon'.

It was well sung, well played, and well received.

Truly poetry is international, just like music,
And falling bombs and death and destruction
And misery and pain and wastage,

Truly we only need one poet in the world
Since local references can be inserted by editors,
Theatre managers or clerks in the Culture Ministries.

Denise Levertov *USA, b. 1923*

AN INTERIM

I
While the war drags on, always worse,
the soul dwindles sometimes to an ant
rapid upon a cracked surface;

lightly, grimly, incessantly
it skims the unfathomed clefts where despair
seethes hot and black.

II

Children in the laundromat
waiting while their mothers fold sheets.
A five-year-old boy addresses
a four-year-old girl. 'When I say,
Do you want some gum? say *yes.*'
'Yes . . .' 'Wait!—Now:
Do you want some gum?'
'Yes!' 'Well yes means no,
so you can't have any.'
He chews. He pops a big, delicate bubble at her.

O language, virtue
of man, touchstone
worn down by what
gross friction . . .

And,
' "It became necessary
to destroy the town to save it,"
a United States major said today.
He was talking about the decision
by allied commanders to bomb and shell the town
regardless of civilian casualties,
to rout the Vietcong.'

O language, mother of thought,
are you rejecting us as we reject you?

Language, coral island
accrued from human comprehensions,
human dreams,

you are eroded as war erodes us.

Jim Burns *UK*

COMMUNIQUE TO A CHILD

First of all you must not complain.
The bomb that blew off your left leg,
and tore away one of your eyes,
was placed by some of our volunteers
to obtain maximum psychological effect
in the struggle to achieve our demands.
It was not our intention to maim
or kill anyone, and we regret the death
of your mother. However, you must
accept that there are no innocents
in a situation such as this.
So, adjust to your present condition,
and do not condemn us. As you
limp into the future your one eye
will enable you to see things clearly,
and you will evaluate the event
with the wisdom of age. You will
begin to understand why it happened.
Only an adult can possibly know this,
and apply reason to the suffering.

Chenjerai Hove *Zimbabwe, b. 1956*

A WAR-TORN WIFE

This war!
I am tired
of a husband who never sleeps
guarding the home or on call-up,
Never sleeping!

Maybe inside him he says
'I am tired of a wife
who never dies
so I could stop guarding.'

Denise Levertov *USA, b. 1923*

WHAT WERE THEY LIKE?

(1) Did the people of Viet Nam
use lanterns of stone?
(2) Did they hold ceremonies
to reverence the opening of buds?
(3) Were they inclined to quiet laughter?
(4) Did they use bone and ivory,
jade and silver, for ornament?
(5) Had they an epic poem?
(6) Did they distinguish between speech and singing?

(1) Sir, their light hearts turned to stone.
It is not remembered whether in gardens
stone lanterns illumined pleasant ways.
(2) Perhaps they gathered once to delight in blossom,
but after the children were killed
there were no more buds.
(3) Sir, laughter is bitter to the burned mouth.
(4) A dream ago, perhaps. Ornament is for joy.
All the bones were charred.
(5) It is not remembered. Remember,
most were peasants; their life
was in rice and bamboo.
When peaceful clouds were reflected in the paddies
and the water buffalo stepped surely along terraces,
maybe fathers told their sons old tales.
When bombs smashed those mirrors
there was time only to scream.
(6) There is an echo yet
of their speech which was like a song.
It was reported their singing resembled
the flight of moths in moonlight.
Who can say? It is silent now.

Jorge Rebelo *Mozambique, b. 1940*

POEM FOR A MILITANT

Mother,
I have an iron rifle
your son,
the one you saw chained
one day
(When you cried as if
the chains bound and battered
your hands and feet)
Your boy is free now
Mother.
Your boy has an iron rifle,
My rifle
will break the chains
will open the prisons
will kill the tyrants
will win back our land
Mother,
Beauty is to fight for freedom,
Justice rings in my every shot
and ancient dreams awaken like birds.
Fighting, on the front,
Your image descends.
I fight for you,
Mother
to dry the tears
of your eyes.

Zulfikar Ghose *Pakistan, b. 1935*

GEOGRAPHY LESSON

When the jet sprang into the sky,
it was clear why the city
had developed the way it had,
seeing it scaled six inches to the mile.
There seemed an inevitability
about what on ground had looked haphazard,
unplanned and without style
when the jet sprang into the sky.

When the jet reached ten thousand feet,
it was clear why the country
had cities where rivers ran
and why the valleys were populated.
The logic of geography—
that land and water attracted man—
was clearly delineated
when the jet reached ten thousand feet.

When the jet rose six miles high,
it was clear that the earth was round
and that it had more sea than land.
But it was difficult to understand
that the men on the earth found
causes to hate each other, to build
walls across cities and to kill.
From that height, it was not clear why.

Chenjerai Hove *Zimbabwe, b. 1956*

EXILED FARMER

Don't close the window
Or curtain it,
For Africa speaks outside:
The splatter of raindrops on the heart
Sings eternal songs:
Would my drummer were here.

The next poem is dedicated to Joy Lowe. She and her husband were South African missionaries who worked for years at the Chiroke Mission in the Eastern Highlands of what was then Rhodesia, until they were deported by Ian Smith's Rhodesian Front government during the Chimurenga War which led to the independent Zimbabwe. The Lowes are close friends of the poet.

The poem that follows after also refers to the Zimbabwean war of independence.

Musaemura Zimunya *Zimbabwe, b. 1949*

THE REASON

To Joy Lowe

In my letter
I feared the loss of love
inside my frame.
Apologies that it shocked you
I was only being frank.
Everyday you see all these men –
prisoners –
misery playing a dead show
in their countenances
laughing unconscious of
the negativeness their voices betray;
some of them too innocent to kill a louse
others too old to know whether they are dead
or alive
the backs of these old men bled
perhaps they gave food to guerilla fighters
I was shown one back: an incomprehensible
tattoo of sjambok tracks showing pink
and this man will be here for five years
a grandad from the backwoods,
he knows not what Rhodesia is,
what Zimbabwe is or what this war is all about!
conscience lambasts you
like a gust of the August wind
disappears like a wisp of cigar smoke
questions unanswered block your thinking
frustration fumes and fumes

Now where is the room
for love?

Chirwa P Chipeya *Zimbabwe*

TODAY

Today
the war
has ended
the people sing
freedom has arrived
the people are singing
songs
of joy or
songs for the dead

Shalom = the Hebrew word for 'Peace'.

Bernard Kops *UK, b. 1926*

SHALOM BOMB

I want a bomb, my own private bomb, my shalom bomb.
I'll test it in the morning, when my son awakes,
hot and stretching, smelling beautiful from sleep. Boom! Boom!
Come my son dance naked in the room.
I'll test it on the landing and wake my neighbours,
the masons and the whores and the students who live downstairs.

Oh I must have a bomb and I'll throw open windows and
count down as I whizz around the living room,
on his bike with him flying angels on my shoulder,
and my wife dancing in her dressing gown.

I want a happy family bomb, a do-it-yourself bomb,
I'll climb on the roof and ignite it there about noon.
My improved design will gong the world and we'll all eat lunch.

My pretty little bomb will play a daytime lullaby and
thank you bomb for now my son falls fast asleep.
My love come close, close, the curtains, my lovely bomb, my
darling,
my naughty bomb. Burst around us, burst between us, burst
within
us. Light up the universe, then linger, linger
while the drone of the world recedes.

Shalom Bomb–

I want to explode the breasts of my wife. Ping! Ping!
In the afternoon and wake everyone,
to explode over playgrounds and parks, just as children
come from schools. I want a laughter bomb,
filled with sherbet fountains, liquorice allsorts, chocolate kisses,
candy floss,
tinsel and streamers, balloons and fireworks, lucky bags,
bubbles and masks and false noses.
I want my bomb to sprinkle the earth with roses.

I want the streets of the world to be filled with crammed,
jammed
kids, screaming with laughter, pointing their hands with wonder,
at my lemonade ice-cream lightning and mouthorgan thunder.
I want a one-man-band bomb. My own bomb.

My live long and die happy bomb, my die peacefully old age
bomb,
in our own beds, bomb.
My Om Mane Padme Hum bomb, my Tiddley Om Pom bomb,
my goodnight bomb, my sleeptight bomb,
my see you in the morning bomb,
I want my bomb, my own private bomb, my Shalom Bomb.

Acknowledgements

Every effort has been made to trace the copyright holders but this has not always been possible. The publisher apologises for any omission of acknowledgement and will amend it in the event of a reprint.

Acknowledgements are due from the editor and the publisher to the following for permission to reprint copyright poems:

Lionel Abrahams and Bateleur Press: 'The Whiteman Blues' from *Thresholds of Tolerance* (Bateleur).

Dannie Abse: 'Driving Home' from *Car Journeys* (Hutchinson); 'Red Balloon' from *Poems, Golders Green* (Hutchinson). ©Dannie Abse. Reprinted by permission of Anthony Sheil Associates Ltd.

Perseus Adams: 'Bird Shrine' from *Grass for the Unicorn* (Juta).

Michael Baldwin: 'Hunting with a Stick' from *How Chas Egget Lost His Way in a Creation Myth* (Secker & Warburg). Copyright © Michael Baldwin.

Shabbir Banoobhai: 'He's a Good Boy, This One' from *Echoes of My Other Self* (Ravan).

Ridley Beeton and Ad. Donker (Pty) Ltd: 'Autumn' and 'On the Beach' from *The Landscape of Requirement* (Ad. Donker).

John Betjeman: 'Executive' from *Collected Poems* (John Murray, Publishers, Ltd).

Elizabeth Bishop: 'The Burglar of Babylon' from *The Complete Poems 1927–1975*. Copyright © 1983 by Alice Helen Methfessel. Copyright © 1964 by Elizabeth Bishop. Renewal Copyright © 1967, 1968, 1971, 1973, 1974, 1975, 1976, 1979 by Elizabeth Bishop. Renewal copyright © 1980 by Alice Helen Methfessel. Originally appeared in *The New Yorker Magazine*. Reprinted by permission of Farrar, Straus and Giroux, Inc.

Edwin Brock and Penguin: 'A Moment of Respect' from *Penguin Modern Poets 8*.

Alan Brownjohn: 'Vital' from *A Song of Good Life* (Secker & Warburg).

Jim Burns: 'Communique to a Child' from *Voices of Today* (The Salamander Imprint).

Charles Causley and Macmillan: 'Timothy Winters' from *Collected Poems* (Macmillan).

Christopher Cheek and Oxford University Press: 'Accident' from *Every Man Will Shout* ed. Roger Mansfield and Isobel Armstrong (1964) © Oxford University Press 1964.

Shimmer Chinodya: 'African Grass' and 'Recollection' from *Zimbabwean Poetry in English* ed. K. Muchemwa (Mambo Press, Gweru, 1978).

Chirwa P Chipeya: 'Today' from *Zimbabwean Poetry in English* (Mambo Press, Gweru, 1978).

Sydney Clouts: 'Firebowl' and 'Roy Kloof' from *Collected Poems* (David Philip). Copyright Marjorie Clouts 1984.

Gregory Corso and New Directions Publishing Corporation: 'Second Night in New York City after Three Years' from *Long Live Man.* Copyright © 1962 by New Directions Publishing Corporation.

Jeni Couzyn: 'In the House of the Father' from *Christmas in Africa,* published in *Life by Drowning* (Anansi, 1983); (Bloodaxe Books, 1985).

Jeremy Cronin: 'Chameleon', 'Visiting Room', 'I saw your Mother' and 'In Blue Bluer-than-any-sea Doeks' from *Inside* (Ravan).

Countee Cullen and Harper & Row, Publishers, Inc.: 'Incident' from *On These I Stand.* Copyright 1927, 1929, 1935, 1945, 1947 by Harper and Brothers.

Patrick Cullinan: 'The Beach, Evening' from *The Horizon Forty Miles Away* (Patrick Cullinan); 'The First, Far Beat' and 'On the Wild Coast' from *The White Hail in the Orchard* (David Philip); 'Madagascar' from *Today is not Different* (Mantis Poets, David Philip).

e e cummings and Grafton Books, a Division of the Collins Publishing Group: 'nobody loses all the time', 'Buffalo Bill's' and 'i thank You God for most this amazing' from *Complete Poems 1913–1962.*

Achmat Dangor: 'Scorn' and 'Paradise' from *Bulldozer* (Ravan).

Jennifer Davids: 'Poem for my Mother' and 'Location Fires' from *Searching for Words* (Mantis Editions, David Philip).

C Day Lewis: 'Walking Away' from *The Gate* (Jonathan Cape). Copyright the Executors of the Estate of C Day Lewis.

Paul Dehn: 'Gutter Press' © Copyright 1965, 1976 Dehn Enterprises Ltd, from *The Fern on the Rock* published by Hamish Hamilton Ltd.

Anthony Delius: 'The Thinker' from *A Corner of the World* (Human & Rousseau).

Modikwe Dikobe: 'Grave of Unknown Whiteman', 'Khoikloi-Son-of-Man' and 'A Night Hawk' from *Dispossessed* (Ravan).

C J Driver: 'White River, Transvaal' and 'In Chapel Street' from *Occasional Light* (Mantis Poets, David Philip).

Douglas Dunn: 'Late Night Walk Down Terry Street'. Reprinted by permission of Faber and Faber Ltd from *Terry Street* by Douglas Dunn.

D J Enright: 'Tourist Promotion' and 'Streets' from *Daughters of Earth* (Chatto & Windus). Reprinted by permission of Watson, Little Ltd.

Lawrence Ferlinghetti and New Directions Publishing Corporation: 'Don't Let that Horse' from *A Coney Island of the Mind* (New Directions). Copyright © 1958 by Lawrence Ferlinghetti.

Michele Freind: 'Days' and 'busstop' from *English Alive 1970* (SACEE).

Estate of Robert Frost and Jonathan Cape Ltd: 'A Time to Talk', 'The Road Not Taken' and 'Out, Out–' from *The Poetry of Robert Frost,* ed. Edward Connery Lathem (Jonathan Cape).

Zulfikar Ghose: 'Geography Lesson' from *Topics in Modern Poetry* (John Murray).

Robert Graves: 'Flying Crooked' from *Collected Poems 1975.* By permission of A P Watt Ltd on behalf of The Executors of the Estate of Robert Graves.

Robert Greig: 'The Race' from *A World of Their Own* ed. Stephen Gray (Ad. Donker)

Mafika Gwala: 'Kwela Ride' and 'One Small Boy Longs for Summer' from *Jol' iinkomo* (Ad. Donker).

Seamus Heaney: 'Follower' and 'Digging' . Reprinted by permission of Faber and Faber Ltd from *Death of a Naturalist* by Seamus Heaney.

A L Hendriks: 'Neighbour, Tenth Floor' from *Madonna of the Unknown Nation* (Workshop Press).

Daniel Hoffman: 'The Center of Attention', Copyright © 1974 by Daniel Hoffman, reprinted from *The Center of Attention* (New York: Random House) by permission of the author.

Chenjerai Hove: 'Exiled Farmer' from *And Now the Poets Speak* (Mambo Press, Gweru, 1981) and 'War-torn Wife' from *Up in Arms* (Zimbabwe Publishing House).

Langston Hughes: 'Mother to Son', from *The Selected Poems of Langston Hughes* (Random House).

Ted Hughes: 'Full Moon and Little Frieda'. Reprinted by permission of Faber and Faber Ltd from *Wodwo* by Ted Hughes.

William Hussey: 'Man Servant' from *Zimbabwean Poetry in English* (Mambo Press, Gweru, 1978).

Wopko Jensma: 'Not Him (3)' and 'Our Village' from *Sing for our Execution* (Ophir/Ravan).

Fhazel Johennesse: 'A Young Man's Thoughts before June the 16th', 'The Nightwatchman', 'The Night Train' and 'Extra' from *The Rainmaker* (Ravan).

Keorapetse Kgositsile: 'The Elegance of Memory' from *Heartprints* (Schwiftinger Galerie-verlag).

Mike Kirkwood and Bateleur Press: 'Neighbours' from *Between Islands* (Bateleur).

Bernard Kops: 'Shalom Bomb' from *Erica, I Want to Read you Something* (Tribune Press).

Mazisi Kunene: 'In Praise of the Ancestors' from *The Ancestors and the Sacred Mountain* (Heinemann Educational Books).

Philip Larkin: 'Days'. Reprinted by permission of Faber and Faber Ltd from *The Whitsun Weddings* by Philip Larkin.

D H Lawrence: 'Self Pity', 'Lizard', 'Baby Running Barefoot', 'Piano', 'Discord in Childhood', and 'Let us be Men' from *The Complete Poems of D H Lawrence.* Reprinted by permission of Laurence Pollinger Ltd and the Estate of Mrs Frieda Lawrence Ravagli.

Hugh Lewin: 'The Wedding' and 'Behind a Barred Window' from *Poets to the People* ed. Barry Feinberg (Heinemann Educational Books).

Douglas Livingstone: 'Gentling a Wildcat'. © Oxford University Press 1970. Reprinted from *Eyes Closed Against the Sun* by Douglas Livingstone (1970) by permission of Oxford University Press; 'Leviathan', 'The King', and 'Pteranodon' from *Sjambok and Other Poems from Africa* (Oxford

University Press); to Douglas Livingstone and Ad. Donker Pty Ltd, 'Dust', 'A Piece of Earth', 'Town Tembu' and 'Veld and Vlei Poem' from *The Anvil's Undertone* (Ad. Donker).

Norman MacCaig: 'Interruption to a Journey' from *Selected Poems* (Chatto & Windus: The Hogarth Press).

Chris Mann: 'In Praise of the Shades' from *First Poems* (Bateleur); 'To Lucky with his Guitar on a Grahamstown Street' from *New Shades* (David Philip).

Don Mattera: 'Remember' and 'For a Cent' from *Azanian Love Song* (Skotaville).

James Matthews: 'The Face of My Mother Takes the Shape' from *No Time for Dreams* (Blac) and 'Trip to Botswana' from *Staffrider.*

Roger McGough: 'My Busconductor' from *Modern Poets 10* (Penguin). Reprinted by permission of A D Peters & Co Ltd.

Stanley Mogobe: 'Two Buckets' from Robert Royston (ed.), *To Whom it May Concern* (Ad. Donker Pty Ltd).

Zulu Molefe: 'Black Zionist Meeting' from Robert Royston (ed.), *To Whom it May Concern* (Ad. Donker Pty Ltd).

Edwin Morgan: 'Good Friday' and 'The Computer's First Christmas Card' from *Poems of Thirty Years* , Carcanet Press Limited, 1982; 'Glasgow 5 March 1971' from *Instamatic Poems,* Ian McKelvie.

Stan Motjuwadi: 'Taken for a Ride' from Robert Royston (ed.), *To Whom it May Concern* (Ad. Donker Pty Ltd).

Casey Motsisi: 'The Efficacy of Prayer' from Robert Royston (ed.), *To Whom it May Concern* (Ad. Donker Pty Ltd).

Mbuyiseni Oswald Mtshali: 'Boy on a Swing' from *Sounds of a Cowhide Drum* (Ad. Donker Pty Ltd).

Charles Mungoshi: 'A Letter to a Son' and 'Christmas' from *Zimbabwean Poetry in English* (Mambo Press, Gweru, 1978).

Arthur Nortje: 'At Lansdowne Bridge' from *Dead Roots.* Published in African Writers Series, Heinemann Educational Books 1973.

Motshile Nthodi: 'Standard Fifty-eight' from *New Classic* (Skotaville); 'Staffrider' from *Staffrider* No. 1 Vol. 1; 'South African Dialogue' from *Quarry 76* (Ad. Donker Pty Ltd).

Alan Paton: 'Dancing Boy' from *Knocking on the Door* (David Philip).

Brian Patten: 'Park Note' from *The Irrelevant Song* (Allen & Unwin).

Lenrie Peters: 'Parachute Men' from *Poems* (Mbari Publications).

Leslie Pickett: 'The One That Got Away' from *Every Man Will Shout* ed. Roger Mansfield and Isobel Armstrong (1964). ©Oxford University Press 1964.

Sylvia Plath: 'You're' from *Collected Poems* (Faber and Faber, London), copyright 1965 and 1967 by Ted Hughes. Reprinted by permission of Olwyn Hughes.

William Plomer: 'To the Moon and Back' from *Collected Poems* (Jonathan Cape Ltd). Reprinted by permission of the Estate of William Plomer.

Henry Pote: 'To a White Child' from *Zimbabwean Poetry in English* (Mambo Press, Gweru, 1978).

Jorge Rebelo: 'Poem for a Militant' from *Ba Shiru* Vol. 1 (1970), translated from Portuguese by Art Brakel. Reprinted by permission of the editors of *Ba Shiru, A Journal of African Languages and Literature,* University of Wisconsin, Madison, Wisconsin 53706, U.S.A. 'Poem' from *When Bullets Begin to Flower* (East African Publishing House).

Richard Rive: 'Where the Rainbow Ends' (*Drum 1955*).

Sol Rochilo: 'The Anonymous Houseboy' from *New Classic 1975* (Skotaville).

Charles Rom: 'How Shall I Tell' from *English Alive 1967* (SACEE).

Damian Ruth: 'When I Go Home' and 'Bezuidenhout' from *Staffrider* Vol. 5 No. 1, 1982.

Carl Sandburg: 'Elephants are Different to Different People' from *The Complete Poems of Carl Sandburg,* Revised and Expanded Edition, copyright 1950 by Carl Sandburg; renewed 1978 by Margaret Sandburg, Helga Sandburg Crile and Janet Sandburg. Reprinted by permission of Harcourt Brace Jovanovich, Inc.

Vernon Scannell: 'Battlefields' from *The Winter Man* (Allison & Busby).

Magoleng wa Selepe: 'My Name' from *Staffrider.*

Sipho Sepamla and Rex Collings, Ltd, London: 'I Saw This Morning' and 'A Wish' from *The Soweto I Love* (Rex Collings).

Sipho Sepamla and Ad. Donker (Pty) Ltd: 'The First Birthday', 'Feeling Small', 'Adriaanspoort' and "To Whom it May Concern' from *Hurry Up to it!* ; 'Da Same, Da Same' from *The Blues is You* (Ad. Donker).

Mongane Serote and Ad. Donker (Pty) Ltd: 'Beerhall Queen' and 'The Actual Dialogue' from *Yakhal' inkomo* (Renoster).

Mutiswayo Shandu: 'Bye Bye, Overcoat' from *Quarry 80–82* (Ad. Donker).

Adam Small: 'Brown Lullaby' and 'Time Signal' from *Kitaar my Kruis* (HAUM).

Gary Snyder: 'Hay for the Horses' from *A Range of Poems* (Fulcrum Press 1966).

Wole Soyinka: 'Telephone Conversation'.

Stephen Spender: 'My Parents Kept Me From Children Who Were Rough'. Reprinted by permission of Faber and Faber Ltd from *Collected Poems* by Stephen Spender.

Elizabeth Spilhaus: 'To Philip' from *English Alive 1968* (SACEE).

Jon Stallworthy and Chatto & Windus: The Hogarth Press: 'The Almond Tree' from *Root and Branch.*

Peter Strauss: 'Bushman Woman Eats a Tsama Melon' from *Photographs of Bushmen* (Bateleur).

Shelley Swade: 'Hey, Beggar' from *English Alive 1969* (SACEE).

Dylan Thomas: 'The Hunchback in the Park' and 'Do not Go Gentle into that Good Night' from *The Poems* (Dent). Reprinted by permission of David Higham Associates Ltd.

Chris van Wyk and Ad. Donker (Pty) Ltd: 'Injustice', 'Catharsis' and 'On Learning Sotho' from *It is Time to Go Home* (Ad. Donker).

Andrew Waterman: 'Mother' from *Livings* (The Marvell Press).

William Carlos Williams: 'The Last Words of My English Grandmother' and 'This is Just to Say' from *Collected Poems, Volume I – 1909–1939*. Copyright 1938 by New Directions Publishing Corporation; 'The Artist' from *Pictures from Brueghel*. Copyright © 1962 by William Carlos Williams. Reprinted by permission of New Directions Publishing Corporation.

Musaemura Zimunya: 'Ask Granpa', 'Cattle in the Rain', 'My Home', 'Old Granny', 'Ifulamachina' and 'The Reason' from *Zimbabwean Poetry in English* (Mambo Press, Gweru, 1978).

Index of poets